Thriving on Stress for Success

Series Editors:
John T. Greer
Donn W. Gresso

Principals Taking
ACTION
Series

A joint publication of
THE NATIONAL ASSOCIATION OF SECONDARY SCHOOL PRINCIPALS
and
CORWIN PRESS, INC.

Rethinking Student Discipline
Alternatives That Work
Paula M. Short, Rick Jay Short and Charlie Blanton

Thriving on Stress for Success
Walter H. Gmelch and Wilbert Chan

Walter H. Gmelch
Wilbert Chan

Thriving on Stress for Success

CORWIN PRESS, INC.
A Sage Publications Company
Thousand Oaks, California

For information address:

Corwin Press, Inc.
A Sage Publications Company
2455 Teller Road
Thousand Oaks, California 91320

SAGE Publications Ltd.
6 Bonhill Street
London EC2A 4PU
United Kingdom

SAGE Publications India Pvt. Ltd.
M-32 Market
Greater Kailash I
New Delhi 110 048 India

Printed in the United States of America

Library of Congress Cataloging-in-Publication Data

Gmelch, Walter H.
    Thriving on stress for success / Walter H. Gmelch, Wilbert Chan.
        p.   cm.   — (Principals taking action)
    Includes bibliographical references and index.
    ISBN 0-8039-6111-1 (cl.)   — ISBN 0-8039-6112-X
    1. School principals—United States—Psychology. 2. Job stress.
I. Chan, Wilbert. II. Title. III. Series.
LB2831.92.G64   1994
371.2′012′0973—dc20   93-37724
                                                          CIP

94 95 96 97 10 9 8 7 6 5 4 3 2 1

Corwin Press Production Editor: Rebecca Holland

Contents

List of Exercises

List of Tables

List of Figures

Preface

Stress intrigues and plagues principals and researchers alike. Internationally, more than 100,000 books, journals, and articles have addressed the phenomenon of stress. Only within the past two decades have we seen the exponential proliferation of articles on the stresses and strains of school administrators (more than 1,000 since 1966). Due to multiple uses, references, conceptualizations, and definitions, the exact meaning of stress remains ambiguous.

This book is intended to bring about greater awareness and visibility of this common menace to principals. It does not represent another general stress management book to be shelved along with the already prolific and popular writings on stress. This book is written for you, the principal, to help you and your school build bridges over the barriers of stress.

Within the management ranks, the superintendent is often popularly identified as the administrator most susceptible to stress and disease. This exclusive assumption, however, remains open to question. For example, we found that principals suffered more severe stress from conflict and time pressures than superintendents did. However, superintendents did experience excessive stress from trying to negotiate with the multiple clients of the school system.

Whether the superintendents or principals suffer the most stress is not the point here. The topics of excessive principal stress and effective performance are the primary concerns of this book. It aims to provide an overview of the most recent ideas on principal stress and to present plans of action for its reduction. To make this presentation meaningful to practicing principals, self-assessment instruments, schematic models, and exercises are used throughout the text to assist you in understanding, internalizing, and applying the key concepts and ideas to make stress a part of your success.

The first step toward stress for success begins by recognizing stress as both a facilitator as well as a debilitator of effective performance. Chapter 1 serves as your personal stress check-up so you can define for yourself what stress is and where it comes from. In Chapter 2 you will explore the myths of administrative stress and identify your stress traps as a principal. Chapter 3 converts these stress traps into plans for action to turn stress from a debilitating enemy to an enabling friend.

The rest of the book explains how stress affects your performance (Chapter 4)—from rustout (Chapter 5) to burnout (Chapter 6)—and how you can maintain high levels of productivity and still keep the competitive edge in your job and in your life (Chapter 7).

The task of recognizing debilitating stress in your life is often difficult and masked by external loci/sources of concern. In addition, once the stress is recognized, there is an even greater challenge to harness its energies and utilize it as a facilitator of success. Nevertheless, hundreds of principals are currently defying the odds leading to burnout and rustout. More important than simply surviving, these principals are moving forward with even greater strides, leaving the question: "How do they do it?"

Hundreds of conversations with school principals over the years have revealed multiple facets of commonality. Most principals work within a traditional school infrastructure that provides supervision and levels of expectations from either the superintendent or assistant superintendent. Many principals must muddle through with an ineffective teacher evaluation process, legalistically designed rather than designed to facilitate professionalism and student success. School districts all over the country are experiencing an explosion of changing demographics. In turn, the burden and pressures of effectively addressing changing needs in the face of shrinking resources often fall on the principal's shoulders. Finally, every school district in the country is facing the burgeoning pressures of school reform. Demands for the creation of site-level managed schools, community and legal pressures for the implementation of outcome based education, struggles with societal demands of the educational enterprise, and the responsibility for school reform measures that effectively guarantee the success of every student are all integral parts of every principal's role and struggle. Understanding the context in which principals operate, how do successful principals cope with the pressures and demands while at the same time gaining additional strength and confidence from their work? We believe they do so by utilizing stress as a facilitator of performance.

Simplistic as it may sound, capturing the pressures of performance is no easy task. Sally Hoskins, a 7-year principal of a large metropolitan high school, recalls:

> I can remember my first year here, I was literally going crazy. The work piled up and I couldn't get out from under the load. I really can't remember how I survived. I felt like giving it up at the end of my first year—it just seemed to be an impossible task. It was at the end of my second year when I finally began to make sense of where some of these pressures were coming from. It was also about that time that my husband said I needed to do something about the responsibilities I was taking on—it was affecting my marriage and role as a mother.

Sally's scenario is not uncommon. At the rate Sally was going, she would have been a prime candidate for professional burnout. The unfortunate reality remains that Sally's burnout would have been a result of her commitment to the job—not her lack of desire.

Thousands of principals across the country are in similar situations. The drive to excel and perform is often the demise of these dedicated principals. The frustration inherent within the system is that it often rewards those principals who are content with the status quo, and brutally punishes those committed to an effective educational process. The time cannot be more appropriate for principals to take back control of their professional lives. In the following pages, you will meet several colleagues who are all committed to educating youth. They work in the type of schools, with the type of staff, and under similar systemic constraints facing each and every one of us. The powerful difference in their performance is their individual ability to recognize the stressor within their lives and to take control of its effects. The lessons we learned are their strategies to effectively utilize performance pressures and stress for personal and professional success. It is a difficult task but not an impossible one—we've seen success happen time and time again. This book was written for those dedicated professionals who understand their commitment and are willing to maximize their performance by focusing their energies toward success rather than simply survival. We wish you the best on your journey.

Walter H. Gmelch
Wilbert Chan

Acknowledgments

This book is based on what we have discovered about stress in school administration both from our research and from practical experiences. The inspiration and information for this book are derived from four main sources: (1) the most current research and writings on stress, including the authors' recent research with Dr. Joe Torelli, investigating the stresses of more than 750 school principals; (2) comments from principals who have attended hundreds of stress workshops using the authors' material; (3) the authors' collective stresses and successes in coping with the pressures of being a teacher, principal, professor, department chair, and corporate executive; and (4) portions of previous writings that have been disseminated in other forms—*Beyond Stress to Effective Management* (1982); *Release From Stress* (University of Oregon OSSC Bulletin, 1981); and "Stress for Success: How to Optimize Your Performance" (*Theory Into Practice*, 1983).

Others have joined us in our endeavor to develop a research base on administrative stress. Specifically, we would like to acknowledge the contribution of Dr. Boyd Swent, Superintendent of Umitilla County ESD, who worked with Walt Gmelch to develop the initial pioneering study in 1977 of stress in Oregon schools. More than 70 studies since that time have used their Administrative Stress Index to explore the sources, reactions, and consequences of administrator stress. Dr. Joe Torelli, Vice Principal of Carmichael Junior High in Washington, directed the 1992 investigation with us to update and expand our knowledge of stress among school administrators.

Our research could not have been possible without the cooperation of thousands of principals who have responded to our studies over the past 15 years. In addition, the practical applications and implications that complement our research emanate from the fine examples we have been fortunate to have as role models and mentors in our professional careers. The encouragement and faith of Donn Gresso and Jack Greer inspired us to first take on this endeavor, and the supportive guidance of Gracia Alkema brought this book to closure. Specifically, Walt Gmelch would also like to thank Ken Erickson, Dale Anderson, Bernie Oliver, George Gmelch, Bill Walsh, Allen Brown, Tuli Glasman, Ed Bridges, Val Miskin, Don Reed, Boyd Swent, and Wilbert Chan for their friendship and inspiration. Wilbert Chan expresses his gratitude to Walt Gmelch, Richard Sagor, Dennis Morrow, James Carroll, and Carol Ericson for their support, encouragement, and insights. Finally, there is no denying the price our families had to pay for the completion of this book. For our wives, Paula and Linda; our boys, Ben, Tom, Joshua, and Casey; we thank you for your understanding and willingness to give us the time.

Most authors write about what troubles them and we are no different. From our burning interest and burned-out experiences, we create the book that follows.

About the Authors

Walter H. Gmelch is Professor and Chair of the Educational Administration Department at Washington State University, where he also serves as Director of the Center for the Study of the Department Chair. An educator, management consultant, university administrator, and former business executive, Gmelch has conducted research and written extensively on the topic of administrator stress and has published more than 50 articles and a dozen books on management, including his classic, *Beyond Stress to Effective Management*. He has been studying stress in school administration since 1977, and in 1992 he completed a comprehensive study of administrator stress with two principals, Wilbert Chan and Joe Torelli. His research has been replicated more than 60 times throughout the United States, Europe, and Asia.

He has presented more than 400 workshops throughout the United States, Asia, Europe, Africa, and Australia to schools, public agencies, universities, colleges, and corporations. He has received numerous honors, including a Kellogg Fellowship, Danforth Leadership Program, Faculty Excellence Award in Research, Australian Research Fellowship, University Council for Educational Administration Distinguished Professor Award, and Education Press Award of America for his monograph titled *Coping With Stress*. He earned a Ph.D. in the Educational Executive Program from the University of California at Santa Barbara, an M.B.A. from the University of California at Berkeley, a B.A. from Stanford University, and an A.A. from the College of San Mateo.

Wilbert Chan is the principal of the Roseville Area Middle School in Roseville, Minnesota. He has traveled and worked extensively throughout Southeast Asia and has both teaching and administrative experience in a variety of educational systems. He received his B.A. from the University of California at Berkeley and his Ph.D. in Educational Administration from Washington State University, where he was the recipient of the Dr. George Brain Leadership Award, the Dorothy B. Cook Scholarship of Excellence, and the Palouse Asian American Scholarship.

Since earning his doctorate, Dr. Chan has continued his research on stress and performance and the principal's role in school culture, as seen through the practitioner's eyes. Additionally, he has presented many workshops in the United States and in Asia, and is the author of "Teacher's Workplace: The Social Organization of Schools," which appeared in the journal *Effective School Report*.

Stress for Success

The Principal's Check-Up

"Sometimes I think I'd be better off if I found another line of work."

The words spoken here are not those of a superintendent squeezed between the board and the educational staff, a teacher overwhelmed by paperwork, or a secretary frustrated from lack of control and recognition; they come from a school principal looking for a new challenge. Within the realm of education, superintendents are popularly identified as those individuals most susceptible to stress, probably because of the nature of their leadership responsibilities. That exclusive assumption, however, is open to question. Principals find themselves caught in the middle, trying to negotiate between school district policy and the sometimes incompatible needs of teachers, staff, and students.

Educational leaders in the twenty-first century will be faced with more pressure, more aggression, more change, and more conflict than in any other period in education. More is crammed into principals' days than ever before, thanks to computers, facsimiles, car and cellular phones, and other *time-saving* devices that have measurably increased the pace of their lives.

No matter what package it comes in, educators recognize the feeling of stress. It plays as much a part in their lives as love, pain, euphoria, and defeat. More than 100,000 books, magazines, and journal articles have been written in the name of stress. Check your neighborhood bookstores—their shelves overflow with self-help psychology, exercise, and nutrition books preaching stress control. Virtually every popular psychology, professional, and airline flight magazine prints one article an issue telling us how to cope with stress. Now journals dedicate entire issues to stress, as is evident from the September 1992 issue of *The School Administrator,* which is totally focused on the stresses of school administration.

What Is Stress?

Good Stress and Bad Stress

Due to multiple uses, references, and definitions, the exact meaning of stress seems ambiguous. Let's begin with the most important definition: your interpretation of stress. Take a minute or two and list below as many one-word synonyms for stress as you can think of. Don't contemplate too long, just write the first words that come to mind.

1.	7.
2.	8.
3.	9.
4.	10.
5.	11.
6.	12.

From Distress to Eustress

Now, reread your one-word definitions. We typically associate with stress the terms *anxiety, frustration, strain,* and the "tension, pressure, pain" we hear from the prolific aspirin commercials. Table 1.1 lists what principals usually say when asked to define stress. You will notice that the words have been subjectively categorized into three columns. The first pertains to the negative stress from the fear,

TABLE 1.1 The Three Faces of Stress

Distress (Negative Stress)	*Stress* (Neutral Stress)	*Eustress* (Positive Stress)
worry	change	success
pressure	issue	promotion
anxiety	conflict	challenge
tension	crisis	opportunity
frustration	noise	progress
aggravation	money	promotion
fear	deadlines	love
annoyance	communication	excitement
troublesomeness	clients	improvement
franticness	criticism	creativity
fatigue	imbalance	friendship
nuisance	discomfort	marriage
trauma	ambiguity	children
confusion	expectations	motivation
strain	schedules	vacation
bewilderment	telephone	achievement
discontent	people	belonging
disappointment	unexpectedness	stimulation

frenzy, and fatigue of everyday living. These emanate from pressure situations, uptight feelings, nervous tensions, personal demands, and other unpleasant encounters.

The second column represents words, attitudes, and behaviors that evoke negative feelings at first but should be considered neutral; that is, if handled properly and put in the right perspective, they could relate to positive experiences as well. Conflict, for example, reminds us of unpleasant encounters with colleagues, but these encounters can also result in positive change, a clearing of the air, innovation, and creativity. Change represents another good example of something that, in moderation, can be the spice of life, but in excess creates aggravation, frustration, and bewilderment.

The third column contains words considered positive or pleasant. They cause stress but in a pleasant manner. Consider your reaction to a promotion or a large salary increase. The excitement you feel psychologically creates a stress reaction much like a cut in pay would. Think back to the last frightful experience you had. Let's say you were driving along the road to work and had to swerve to avoid a head-on collision. How would your body react?—fast heartbeat, increased blood pressure, eyes dilating, rapid breathing, sweaty palms, and so on. Now think back to a very pleasurable experience. How about the day you received tenure?—fast heartbeat, sweaty palms, eyes dilating, rapid breathing, and so on.

So you see, whether stress is positive or negative, your initial physiological reaction is much the same. In essence, stress is any event that places a demand on your body, mentally or physically. Notice the similarity in all stress, whether positive or negative. With our tendency to emphasize the negative effects of stress, we have forgotten to look at the duality of stress. The Chinese use two characters when spelling stress: The first signals *danger* and the other *opportunity*. Like the Chinese representation, we also have words in our language to express both feelings: *distress* for bad or unpleasant events, and *eustress* for good or pleasant. Through slurring, the old Middle English word *distress* came into common English usage as "stress." Eustress came from the Greek prefix of *eu* meaning good, as in *euphoria*. You will be reminded throughout this book to change your view of stress from negative—something to rid yourself of—to one of balance: to recognize and use positive effects of stress to your advantage. Your stress reduction strategy should be to minimize your negative stress factors and maximize the positive ones.

The Sources of Stress: Your Stress Check-Up

Where does stress come from? Nearly 2,000 years ago an emperor of China posed a similar question to his physician: "Does not the troublesome wind cause illness?" Whatever the language and wherever the place, nature—through the forces of wind, cold, and heat—has brought about tension, depression, headaches, and other illnesses.

Even more catastrophic than the stresses of nature are those created in the schools themselves. These stresses are found in all aspects of being a principal, from the school environment, the nature of principals' work, the educators they work with to those within their own

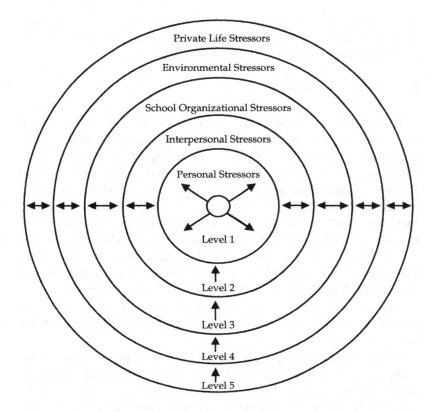

Figure 1.1. Levels of Principal Stress

personalities and dispositions. The five levels of stress in Figure 1.1 represent these potential areas of principal stress.

The levels of stress, descending from the environment down to the principal's idiosyncrasies, are reviewed in that order. This sequence is more expedient than real since significant stressors can attack at any level, in any direction, or in any unpredictable manner, shifting from level to level. As you read through each succeeding section, become cognizant that stress is cumulative; although one disturbing event during the day may not be enough to reactivate an ulcer, a series of stressors over a short period of time (or several prolonged stressors) becomes synergistic and calamitous to your productivity and, even more important, to your health. Locked in as stress prisoners, the only salvation for principals is to begin to get control over their lives and learn the strategies of coping.

Level 1: Personal Stressors

The same sources of stress provoke different reactions in different principals. Your susceptibility to stress is determined by both genetic and developmental characteristics. A great deal of research has been conducted to try to determine the relationship between different people's dispositions and their consequent vulnerability to stress-related illnesses. The classic experiments were begun 30 years ago by two research cardiologists, Meyer Friedman and Ray Rosenman (1974), who found that a group of tax accountants' cholesterol levels rose as the April 15 tax deadline approached and fell after the deadline passed. Further studies by Friedman and Rosenman showed distinctive Type A and Type B personalities, the former being more susceptible to high blood pressure and increased cholesterol levels, which contribute to the ultimate stress-related illness, coronary heart disease.

Principals exhibiting Type A behavior are typically aggressive, competitive, impatient, hostile to frustration, and possess a strong sense of time urgency. The school setting always seems to act as a trigger to bring out Type A behaviors. Type B's are exactly the opposite; they are rarely harried, able to relax without feeling guilty, and work without agitation.

Who are the Type A's? Middle-class business executives? Not necessarily so. Type A behavior is common among all occupations, ages, classes, and sexes. In fact, 60% of the people Friedman and Rosenman studied were classified as Type A personalities. If you score 8 to 10 on the "personal" section in Exercise 1.1 at the end of this chapter, you may have Type A tendencies.

Are Type A's more successful than B's? Do they tend to hold high positions in their organizations? Once again Friedman and Rosenman believe that most high-level executives are not necessarily Type A's. In fact, many executives reach their levels of success through steady, confident, secure Type B behavior. In our studies of school administrators, we found a greater tendency for principals to exhibit

Type A behaviors than superintendents (Gmelch, Chan, & Torelli, 1992).

It is true that Type A people work hard and fast to succeed, constantly set and strive toward goals, and are highly achievement-oriented, pushing themselves to near capacity. But while they may receive their rewards, they live by dangerously unhealthy rules, and the odds are three times greater for them that coronary heart disease will be the ultimate victor.

Level 2: Interpersonal Stressors

The second level of stress, the interpersonal, is so evident and common that it needs little explanation. Relationships can either make your work pleasurable or make it miserable. Principals strive to perfect the art of identifying and resolving conflict situations, both positive and negative. Conflict resolution represents a major part of a principal's job, since stress exists whenever people work together in organized settings.

Good working relationships, according to several behavioral scientists, contribute to a healthy work environment. A healthy working relationship depends on support, trust, and cooperation. The Goddard study at NASA (Cooper & Marshall, 1976) found poor relationships, defined as low trust, low support, and low interest in listening, produced low job satisfaction and the feeling of being threatened— or psychological stress. Several other studies found that mistrust led to poor communication and strain.

How about the interaction with your teachers, staff, and students? Assess your ability to work with people in Exercise 1.1 at the end of this chapter.

Level 3: School Stressors

Stress from the school setting is characterized by factors that reflect the organization itself (size, number of students and staff, rules and regulations) as well as factors that relate to position and interaction of people (role conflict, job ambiguity).

Stress levels are not the same for all school districts and vary from school to school. If you were to develop lists of high stress and low stress schools, they would include both successful and unsuccessful school settings. Attention should be given not to naming the schools, but to the reasons why they are particularly stressful. Most of the reasons fall into the following categories: lack of clear standards, lack of security, unreasonable demands, dismissals, financial difficulty, new central office and building management, hard-driving management, unrealistic expectations, and so on.

Specifically, what makes one school more stress engendering than another depends on the predominance of certain properties: work overload, underwork, job ambiguity, organizational structure, role conflict, difficult people, transportation difficulties, educational change or restructuring. The following outlines the evidence behind each of these properties.

1. *Work Overload:* Excessive and inconvenient hours, tasks "over one's head," and constant deadlines all contribute to poor mental and physical health. Having too difficult or too much work to do creates stress, the former being qualitative overload and the latter quantitative overload, both topics elaborated upon further in Chapters 3 and 4.

Qualitative overload occurs when discrepancies exist between professional preparation and actual work assignments. In one study, a group of middle-class background, college-educated individuals hired as managers experienced less illness than a second group who had not completed college but were promoted to managerial positions. Similarly, Cornell University researchers found more illness among workers whose family and education were inconsistent with their occupation than among those whose social background and aspirations coincided with their employment. Clearly, administrative training and certification are important components in preparing principals to accept the challenge and respond to the stress generated by the schools.

Quantitative overload correlates highly with a number of symptoms or indicators of stress: cigarette smoking, escapist drinking, absenteeism from work, and lowered self-esteem.

In sum, work overload, both qualitative and quantitative, has been shown to produce at least a dozen different symptoms: job dissatisfaction, lower self-esteem, increased feelings of being threatened, increased drinking, absenteeism, lower motivation, embarrassment, increased smoking, increased heart rate, higher cholesterol levels, and job tension.

2. *Underwork:* Relieving overwork by doing less sometimes provides an agreeable release, but in the long run being underworked leads to dissatisfaction, doubting of one's abilities, and demoralization. Although fewer studies have been conducted that support the "underload" hypothesis, Tobias Brocher, psychiatrist for the Menninger Foundation's Educational Programs on Human Behavior, contends that most frustrations of young managers stem from unfulfilling or unchallenging jobs, not work overload (McGrath, 1976b). Regardless of this less scientific verdict, we would generally concur that a principal with an unfulfilled need for achievement may suffer from job tension. In Chapters 3 and 4 we explore the relationship between under-/overwork and principals' performance.

3. *Job Ambiguity:* All too often principals are left unsure of the scope of their responsibilities; they simply do not know where their job begins and ends. They find themselves in an ever-expanding role, continually facing increased demands from the community, central office, teachers, staff, and students. With the advent of collective bargaining, accountability, downward fiscal trends, legal overload, and new state and federally mandated programs, and the increasing number of court decisions affecting schools, principals' responsibilities can easily become ambiguous and excessive.

Inadequate information about job responsibilities, scope, and objectives, as well as colleagues' expectations, contribute to stress indicators of depression, low self-esteem, life and job dissatisfaction, futility, and intention to leave the job.

4. *Organizational Structure:* Another potential source of stress stems from the structure of schools: the presence of hierarchies, lack of participative decision-making, and omnipotence of rules. One example of hierarchies comes from the old Prussian army organization, where a chain of command was essential to instill order in times of war. The twentieth-century behavioral scientist Chris Argyris contends, however, that it is unnatural to have people stacked atop one

another in an organizational pyramid (Argyris, 1971). This especially holds true in such professional organizations as schools, hospitals, and universities. In fact, the number of hierarchical levels positively correlates with job tension and conflict. One study indicated that 83% of the staff experienced a great deal of dysfunctional conflict when there were six to seven levels between teachers and supervisors, contrasted with a 14% indication of conflict in an organization with only three levels between teachers and supervisors (Corwin, 1969).

The recent trend toward site-based management seems to make good sense both practically and empirically. Research relevant to business' participatory management concept centers around the issue of decision making. According to the Goddard study, employees with greater opportunities to participate in decision making experienced higher feelings of self-esteem and job satisfaction and lower feelings of job-related threat (Cooper & Marshall, 1976). Another study reported that nonparticipation was the most consistent and significant predictor of stress and strain on the job. Under more autocratic chief executives, managers felt pressure and strain because they were unable to complete the work in their own way (Margolis, Kroes, & Quinn, 1974).

With respect to school structure and stress-producing conflict, a number of research findings suggest that (1) the more heterogeneous a staff, the greater the conflict (people like to be with others of similar background and interests); (2) the greater the degree of specialization by departments, the greater the conflict (specialization encourages competition between departments); (3) the higher the interdependence among educators, the greater the conflict (it is more difficult to coordinate work with others than to work independently); (4) the more closely principals supervise, the greater the conflict (people become uneasy when others look over their shoulders); and (5) the greater the school structure in terms of rules, the less the interpersonal conflict and the greater the intrapersonal conflict (more rules define territories for teachers and principals but inhibit personal creativity). Not all conflict is negative, but it does cause stress and must be dealt with creatively.

5. Role Conflict: Teachers, students, and community members of a school may hold quite different role expectations for the principal. If these expectations differ from activities actually performed by the principal, he or she will experience a psychological conflict. Such conflict often occurs when simultaneous expectations are placed on a person, and compliance to one would be in conflict with the satisfaction of the other. A superintendent may make it clear to the principals that they are expected to closely supervise the teaching staff; the teachers, on the other hand, feel supervision should be loosely administered because they are all professionals.

Research again provides consequential evidence of role conflict: Being torn between two groups expecting different kinds of behavior psychologically manifests high tension and low satisfaction and physically contributes to coronary heart disease and obesity (excessive weight for age and height).

6. Managing People: Managers typically spend their days behind desks, writing, calling, and talking to others. Those whose work involves physical activity have lower incidence of stress-related illnesses (for example, coronary heart disease) than sedentary managers. One would think this is largely due to results from the physical inactivity of management positions, but it is also related to managers' "responsibility for people." A principal's responsibility for people means attending meetings, interacting with others, adhering to deadlines, fulfilling personal commitments, and faithfully executing reports, memos, and projects, all of which involve interpersonal dependence. This line of work leads to a higher rate of heart disease than work where one is responsible for things (equipment, supplies, budgets, and the like). This is not to say a computer programmer does not become frustrated when a program aborts; however, the solution is usually logical, whereas resolving conflicts with people in schools may not be so straightforward. Ultimately, responsibility for people, as opposed to inanimate objects, correlates significantly to heavy smoking, high blood pressure, and high cholesterol levels: all important stress warning signals.

7. Travel: The average principal typically lives in the community where he or she works, drives a short distance to the school, and proceeds through the day in a familiar routine. Interrupting this day-to-day pattern with conferences, workshops, or day-long meetings often provides a potentially exciting and stimulating alternative. However, once the distances become greater and more frequent, these changes become an irritant to a stable daily routine. With today's more efficient modes of transportation and mechanization, people expect to be in more places and do more than ever before.

8. The Nature of Educational Change and Restructuring: Much of the stress principals experience is due to educational changes in the past decade. The reform and restructuring movements guarantee that the only stability in education is change: involvement by students in decisions that affect them, growth of citizen activism, site-based management, mandates from federal and state governments, and change for the sake of change.

The preceding eight school organizational stressors are not exhaustive, nor are they reported in high to low stress-producing order. Others could be added.

Level 4: Environmental Stressors

Many environmental stressors are so commonplace that you may be unaware of their impact. Temperature, wind, rain, and changes in weather are obvious contributors. Overpopulated cities burdened with crowds to maneuver through, lines to stand in, seats to fight for, faceless bureaucracies to deal with, and meaningless noise to listen to can cause environmental stress attacks. Studies have found causal relationships between stress and seating arrangements, room design, territorial behavior, noise density, and so on. Noise, for example, plagues teachers and students in shops, P.E. classes, recesses, lunch periods, and offices, producing side effects such as dizziness, decreases in gastric functions, visual disabilities, fatigue, headaches, and nausea. These, in turn, contribute to poor job performance and absenteeism by students and staff.

Not all noise causes adverse consequences. Much depends on how it is perceived. The sound of a joyous staff party plays like music to a principal's ears, but such frolic transferred to a quiet library setting creates a different response. Noise generally disturbs us most when it is inappropriate or unpredictable.

Office furnishings can also create more discomfort than ease. The placement of a principal's desk, for instance, is crucial. By unconsciously locating the desk in the middle of the room (putting it between you and your visitors), psychological distance is created and a superior-inferior relationship is implied; obviously, this is not as conducive to relaxed interaction as placing the desk against a wall with a window (for natural light), allowing you to greet visitors without a desk between you. Sitting behind the desk in an orthopedically unsound, cushiony executive swivel chair for sustained periods tends to aggravate an already aching back. According to researchers, even working all day under fluorescent lighting creates more tension and fatigue than working under lighting that approximates morning sunlight.

Probably the most stress-producing office practice is the open-door policy—the belief that other people own your time. This notion was reinforced by a principal who suggested that "an efficient and effective organization has an open-door policy. . . . When the door is open, even when other people are present, anyone is welcome." The spirit of that policy may be better construed to mean that people should be accessible but not incessantly available to all. Physically leaving the door open just invites interruptions from those corridor wanderers who have nothing better to do than take up your time. It results in an incrementally interrupted day, which eventually wears down one's patience. The trouble with patience is, the more one has, the more people want to use. In sum, environmental stress is not so much a matter of the stressors themselves but of your ability to control them.

Level 5: Private Life Stressors

Crises principals experience rarely relate directly to the tensions and pressures of the job alone. Stressors from outside the school directly impact effectiveness. These pressures stem from demands placed on time, energy, and commitment by families, friends, community, leisure, and other spheres of your private life outside the realm of the principalship.

Many clinical psychologists agree that problems at home can cause more anxiety in the office than discipline and staff problems can. Even pressures attributed to school circumstances are sometimes triggered by home concerns. The head of an employee assistance program for a worldwide clothing firm testifies that most executives initially seek help about some specific work-related problem (personnel conflicts, work overload), but what really bothers them are the external pressures from personal and family problems. In fact, a National Institute of Mental Health study identified 10 "life strains" linked directly to feelings of anxiety and depression. Only five deal with occupational problems, while three relate to marriage and two to parenting (Yankelovich, Shelley, & White, 1982, p. 24).

In other words, the job creates enough tension, but when we add the demands on our time and energy from our private lives, stress snowballs and at times becomes overwhelming. A letter from the new principal in a prominent school typifies this dilemma:

> The job of managing a school is a cinch. The job of being a mother at age 42 to a new baby girl is also a cinch. The job of renovating a new house and garden is still a cinch. The task of doing those three together is well beyond me.

Many of us feel the same way. We must be aware of the pressures from outside our work environment, keep them in perspective, realize the impact they can have on our job performance, and learn to manage the stress in our private, as well as professional, lives.

Within these levels, what causes you the greatest stress? Does most of your stress attack from any particular level? Are you your own worst enemy, or are your greatest pressures environmental and beyond your control? To answer these questions, take a few minutes and fill out the questionnaire in Exercise 1.1. It will help you assess the areas of stress most likely to cause you concern. View the questions as suggestive, not definitive. The intent is to provide an overview of some of the stressors within each of the five spheres of your life.

Exercise 1.1

Assessing Stressors

Completing this exercise can help you determine the pattern of your potential stressors. Place a check in the appropriate column for each item.

Private Life

Agree   Disagree

_____   _____   1. I find myself unable to fulfill my community responsibilities.

_____   _____   2. I cannot find time to complete my projects at home.

_____   _____   3. I often feel that nothing else matters in life besides being a principal.

_____   _____   4. My family/friends would like me to spend more time with them.

_____   _____   5. I would like to develop a hobby but cannot find the time.

_____   _____   6. I rarely socialize with anyone besides other educators.

_____   _____   7. My devotion to work is usually in conflict with my devotion to family and friends.

_____   _____   8. I have a difficult time making financial ends meet.

_____   _____   9. I am concerned about crime and danger in my school and community.

_____   _____   10. Family problems often concern me (e.g., trouble with children, marriage, illness).

_____   _____   Subtotal

Environmental

Agree   Disagree

_____   _____   1. My office is unorganized and too crowded.

_____   _____   2. It sometimes gets too hot or cold in my office.

_____   _____   3. The lighting is inadequate in my office.

_____   _____   4. My office is abnormally noisy.

_____	_____	5. The furniture and/or equipment do not facilitate relaxation and easy interaction with others.
_____	_____	6. Telephones and other interruptions frequently stop what I am doing.
_____	_____	7. My office door is usually open to drop-in visitors.
_____	_____	8. The office equipment does not work properly.
_____	_____	Subtotal

Organizational

Agree	Disagree	Overload
_____	_____	1. There seems to be a sense of urgency about all tasks.
_____	_____	2. I have more work than I can complete in a normal working day.
_____	_____	3. My responsibilities are difficult to keep up with.
_____	_____	4. There is constant pressure to work every minute, with little opportunity to relax.
_____	_____	5. I frequently spend evenings and weekends finishing my work or attending school activities.
_____	_____	6. I find it difficult to keep up with the journals and developments in education.
_____	_____	Subtotal

Agree	Disagree	Underload
_____	_____	1. My job is seldom challenging.
_____	_____	2. I frequently find my work boring and repetitive.
_____	_____	3. I feel my skills and abilities are not being used well.
_____	_____	4. My work is often not very complex.
_____	_____	5. I seldom feel a sense of accomplishment because I cannot see the final product of what I do.
_____	_____	6. I am given very little responsibility.
_____	_____	Subtotal

Agree	Disagree	Job Ambiguity
_____	_____	1. My job responsibilities are generally vague, unclear, and inconsistent.
_____	_____	2. I am not sure I have divided my time properly among tasks.
_____	_____	3. There is little opportunity to receive feedback on how I am doing.
_____	_____	4. Explanations of what has to be done are often unclear.
_____	_____	5. My goals and objectives are intangible and not clearly spelled out.
_____	_____	6. I am not sure how much authority I have.
_____	_____	Subtotal

Agree	Disagree	School Structure
_____	_____	1. I have little direct contact with my superintendent/supervisor.
_____	_____	2. An overabundance of rules and policies do not allow me the freedom to make my own decisions or use my ideas.
_____	_____	3. There is great pressure for all teachers and staff to dress, behave, and think alike.
_____	_____	4. New laws and school codes frequently require me to change the way I do things.
_____	_____	5. The central office is unreceptive to the needs at the building level.
_____	_____	Subtotal

Agree	Disagree	Role Conflict
_____	_____	1. I am often caught between conflicting demands from the central office and the teachers.
_____	_____	2. I receive assignments without adequate staff and resources to carry them out.
_____	_____	3. I often feel pressure to spend both more time at work and more time with my family and friends.
_____	_____	4. I often have difficulty deciding between high productivity and high quality.

_____ _____ 5. I sometimes feel I have to do things to succeed in my work which are in conflict with my basic values.

_____ _____ 6. Things I do are often accepted by one person and not another.

_____ _____ Subtotal

Agree   Disagree   Managing People

_____ _____ 1. I am too often meeting with my staff and do not have enough time to myself.

_____ _____ 2. I often have to make decisions affecting the lives of students and employees.

_____ _____ 3. I often have to consult other people before making a decision.

_____ _____ 4. I sit most of the day and try to get tasks done through other people.

_____ _____ 5. I rarely have the opportunity to manage rational, logical, and objective things (budgets, equipment, and the like).

_____ _____ 6. I often feel today's students and teachers lack the motivation and pride to do a good job.

_____ _____ Subtotal

Agree   Disagree   Travel Away From the School

_____ _____ 1. My job frequently takes me out of town while work piles up on my desk in the office.

_____ _____ 2. I find that I am expected to travel greater distances more frequently.

_____ _____ 3. I frequently find myself traveling on the weekends, late evenings, and early mornings.

_____ _____ 4. Due to travel demands, my daily routine and family time are frequently interrupted.

_____ _____ 5. I commute long distances to and from work.

_____ _____ Subtotal

Interpersonal

Agree   Disagree

_____ _____ 1. My colleagues seldom get together socially.

_____	_____	2. I frequently have to confront students and staff members on an individual basis.
_____	_____	3. My colleagues and I seldom talk together about personal problems.
_____	_____	4. We more often compete with one another than cooperate with a feeling of team spirit.
_____	_____	5. I generally do not get along well with those whose opinions differ greatly from mine.
_____	_____	6. My colleagues generally do not have much interest in what I do.
_____	_____	7. I often have difficulty eliciting support from my other principals and teachers.
_____	_____	8. There often seems to be a lack of trust between myself and my staff.
_____	_____	9. I often feel my job is threatened by my teachers.
_____	_____	10. My superintendent/supervisor often deals with me in an autocratic and overdemanding manner.
_____	_____	Subtotal

Personal

Agree	Disagree	
_____	_____	1. I am frequently in a hurry.
_____	_____	2. I am typically doing several things at the same time.
_____	_____	3. When someone takes too long to get to the point, I usually hurry him or her along.
_____	_____	4. I have a hard time delegating tasks because others cannot complete the tasks as well as I can.
_____	_____	5. I often become discouraged when I compare "who I am" to "who I hoped to be" at this time/stage in my life.
_____	_____	6. I often feel that I have not met my life's ambitions because of my own inadequacies.
_____	_____	7. I often find it hard to focus on any one activity for a long period of time (more

than 10 minutes) because of competing
demands on my time.

_____ _____ 8. I often feel compelled to be successful
because I have been in the past, and now
others expect it of me.

_____ _____ 9. I often believe I am successful because I
can get things done faster than others.

_____ _____ 10. I am meticulously careful about all the
details of my job.

_____ _____ Subtotal

Now that you have completed Exercise 1.1, review each of the
statements with which you have agreed and fill out the chart on
page 21. Be aware of the cumulative effects of stress; although one
disturbing event during the day may not be enough to reactivate an
ulcer, a series of stressors over a short period (or several prolonged
stressors) detracts from your productivity and, even more important, your health.

Generally, if you agreed with 20 to 40 items, your prospects for
realizing tremendous gains on stress by completing this book are
excellent. If you agreed with more than 40, the same is true, but your
road to success may be a bit more difficult. Anyone with a score of
less than 20 must already be on the road to success and conscious
of effective stress-reducing practices.

If you agreed with more than half the questions in any one of the
areas, you should set stress reduction in that area as your primary
target. Take the level of stress with the highest percentage of stress
responses (see column 4 of the Summary chart) and write the level
in the center or bull's-eye of your Stress Target diagram in Exercise
1.2. Take your next highest percentage level and place it in the
second concentric circle.

Continue in the same manner until you have filled in the Stress
Target from the center to the outer ring. You now have a visualization of what you should be shooting for in your attack on stress.

Summary of Stressor Scores

List below your subtotal scores for each of the categories in Exercise 1.1.

	(1) Agree	(2) Disagree	(3) Total	(4) Percent Agreed Items (Column 1÷ Column 3)
Private Life	_____	_____	10	_____
Environmental	_____	_____	8	_____
Organizational				
Overload	_____	_____	6	_____
Underload	_____	_____	6	_____
Job Ambiguity	_____	_____	6	_____
School Structure	_____	_____	5	_____
Role Conflict	_____	_____	6	_____
Managing People	_____	_____	6	_____
Travel	_____	_____	5	_____
Interpersonal	_____	_____	10	_____
Personal	_____	_____	10	_____
Total	_____	_____	78	_____

Interaction of Stressors

Central to Figure 1.1, the diagram of Levels of Principal Stress, introduced at the beginning of this section, is a person's unique disposition (Level 1) to other stressors (Levels 2, 3, 4, and 5). A person's personality is important in determining his or her responses to external, environmental, organizational, and interpersonal stressors. These potential sources of stress are always present, but it is the interaction of stressors that determines whether a situation will be stressful. The five levels of stressors can be thought of as independent spheres constantly in motion, overlapping at times and at other times isolated. If the levels of stress shift so that no overlap exists between the personal level and any of the other four levels, no physical or psychological reactions will occur. It is, therefore, the interaction between your personality and other levels that determines stressful behavior, the key to stress for success. Also, trade-offs between the personal demands and those on the job—with the goal of becoming a holistic principal—will help balance your personal and professional lives.

Exercise 1.2

Target Your Stress

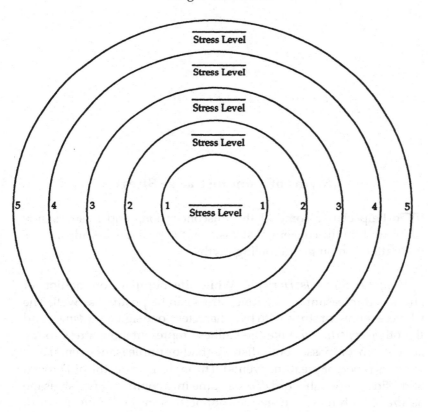

2

Principals' Stress

Myths of Administrative Stress

To help clarify some of the misconceptions and misuses surrounding the concept of stress over the past few decades, focus your attention on the following myths.

Myth #1: Stress Is Harmful. While the popular connotation of stress is unpleasant or negative, stress can be positive as well. The Chinese represent stress with two characters, one signaling *danger* and the other *opportunity.* Like the Chinese representation, stress today actually encompasses both distress (bad or unpleasant events) and eustress (good or pleasant events). Through slurring, the old French and Middle English word *distress* came into common English usage as *stress,* with its sole negative connotation in the Western world. Failure is stressful, but so is success.

Myth #2: Stress Should Be Avoided. Stress is a natural part of life and helps individuals respond to threat or rise to challenge. In essence, it cannot and should not be avoided, for without stress you could not live. To be under stress actually means that you are under *excessive*

stress or distress. An analogous condition is that of running a temperature, meaning above normal. Body temperature itself is essential to
life, just as is stress. Stress cannot be avoided, other than by death.
Therefore, principals should not always seek to avoid stress; it can
be the spice of life, when handled right.

Myth #3: The Higher up in the Organization, the Greater the Stress. It
is popularly believed that high-level executives lead the list of heart
disease patients. However, a Metropolitan Life Insurance Company
study challenged this assumption when it found that presidents and
vice presidents of the 500 largest industrial corporations suffered
40% fewer heart attack deaths than did middle managers of the same
companies. Similar data support the conclusion that middle managers
have a higher peptic ulcer rate than do chief executive officers.

Myth #4: Stress Is a Male-Dominated Phenomenon. Until the 1980s
the literature commonly referred to "men under stress." While this
misguided reference no longer prevails, it is a well-known fact that
men suffer higher rates of alcoholism, ulcers, lung cancer, suicide,
and heart disease than women. However, as the number of women
in male-dominated professions increases, so do incidents of stress
and stress-related diseases. In a study of principals, women principals reported less stress than men (Gmelch, Chan, & Torelli, 1992).

Myth #5: There Is One Right Way to Cope With Stress. Researchers
have addressed popular and academic concerns as well as concep-
tual, theoretical, and empirical investigations on coping, and the
answer to effective coping processes remains elusive. Given the
recent interest in educator stress, it is surprising to find little attention is given to the precise ways educators cope with stress.

Identifying Your Stress Traps

Setting the Stage

What does a principal's typical day consist of? The following
scenario may depict what a principal does on any given day.

The morning begins with the sound of the alarm, a hurried breakfast, a quick kiss to spouse and kids, and the harried push-and-shove commute to the school, just in time to arrive prior to the faculty and students. If the principal is lucky, the early arrival permits a cursory perusal of the day's tasks, commitments, and committee meetings.

Planning time is abruptly interrupted by the onslaught of urgent calls, crises, or calendar changes. Five cups of coffee, four teacher drop-ins, three committee meetings, two irate parents, and one call from the superintendent later, the principal realizes that it's time to grab a sack lunch and gobble it down on the way to the next activity.

The afternoon is productive but hectic, saved by the dismissal bell, which signals the beginning of relatively quiet contemplation time. But alas, a parent conference, a faculty emergency, and a student discipline problem have all crowded into the principal's late afternoon schedule.

In the evening family commitments come second to the endless school and community meetings, clubs, and social events that a principal is expected to attend. Monday through Friday are spent reacting to the urgent demands of parents, teachers, students, and central office; while Saturdays, Sundays, and evenings seem to be the only times a principal can keep up with the paperwork and/or ponder future plans in a more proactive rather than reactive way.

Principals love people, and that is why they are principals, but the stress headache and activated peptic ulcer at the end of a frenzied day make them wonder whether being a principal isn't hazardous to their health.

The Stress Log

A necessary precursor to managing stress is to recognize the stress that occurs in your day and acknowledge that something must be done to reduce it. If you agree on this central point, then take the first positive step and consciously identify the sources of stress. The stress log in Exercise 2.1 represents the most helpful tool to identify what troubles you as a principal.

Exercise 2.1

Stress Log

Stress can come from a single dramatic incident (Isolated Stress), or from a cumulation of less dramatic related incidents (Synergistic Stress).

For one week, at the end of each working day, describe:

1. The most stressful single incident that occurred on your job (confronting a staff member, and so on).
2. The most stressful series of related incidents that occurred on your job (frequent telephone interruptions, and so on).
3. How your day went. Indicate from "1" (not very stressful) to "10" (very stressful) the approximate level of your stress for each day.

	1. Single Incident	2. Series	3. Daily Stress Level
Monday Date:			
Tuesday Date:			
Wednesday Date:			
Thursday Date:			
Friday Date:			

Indicate below other stressful incidents that usually occur but did not take place during this particular week.

1.

2. etc.

The log is based on the assumption that we can mentally perceive what is bothering us, without relying on such physiological devices as biofeedback or galvanic skin response instruments. While the task of assessing what stresses us through self-perception is difficult, the stress log represents a useful tool to accomplish this goal.

Record stresses in your log for at least a 2-week period.

After you have kept the log for a week, read over your list of stressors and add at the bottom of the log any other stressful situations that usually occur but for some reason did not during this particular week. Then, review your entire log and see if certain stress traps reappeared several times. If so, is there a pattern to their recurrence? For example, do you find yourself consistently plagued by drop-in visitors? Or are you troubled by staff blowups and conflicts? If so, what can you generalize about the sources of these stress traps?

Do not forget to reflect on your scores in Column 3. What kind of week did you have? Did most of your daily stress levels rise to the 7-to-10-point range? What is your average daily stress level for the week?

Follow these first week reflections with a second week's stress log. Some new troublesome stressors may surface from this log. You may also begin to see possible patterns or cycles of stress traps. Did you find Tuesdays bogged down with too many and too inefficient meetings? Are Thursdays fraught with conflict at faculty meetings? Are some days typically more stressful than others?

Use your stress logs to note all the different kinds and sources of administrative stress, as well as to observe their daily patterns and weekly cycles. If you find your work repetitive and predictable, your stressors will follow the same pattern, not only daily and weekly but also monthly, quarterly, and yearly. Figure 2.1 shows the actual stress patterns from a study of elementary and secondary teachers and principals. Do you notice the sharp rises in stress from starting and finishing certain cycles in the academic year? Your pattern may be similar.

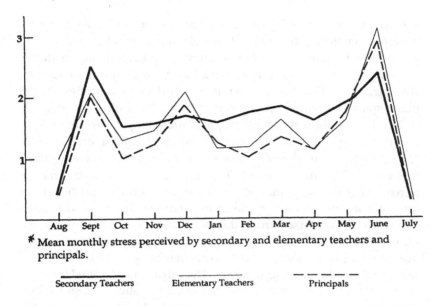

* Mean monthly stress perceived by secondary and elementary teachers and principals.

| Secondary Teachers | Elementary Teachers | Principals |

Figure 2.1. Stress Patterns in Schools

The Administrative Stress Index

Most principals would protest that a 1- or 2-week log may not produce a comprehensive listing of all potential stress traps. The data from your log, coupled with the Administrative Stress Index (ASI), fulfills this purpose (Gmelch & Swent, 1984).

The Administrative Stress Index was developed from several sources. First, 70 administrators were asked to keep stress logs much the same as you did in Exercise 2.1. Next, a survey was conducted of educational administration job descriptions, in search of additional components not already mentioned in the 70 logs. Finally, other instruments purporting to assess occupational stress were investigated for additional items. The compilation of items from all three sources resulted in the Administrative Stress Index. Over the past 15 years the ASI has been used in more than 100 studies of school principals.

We will share what the researchers say about principals' stress in the next section of this chapter; but for now, take a moment and assess your own stress by using the ASI in Exercise 2.2. As you read through each item, rate it from "1" (rarely or never bothers you) to "5" (frequently bothers you). After you have responded to all the items, review your stress logs in Exercise 2.1 and search for other specific stress traps not listed in the ASI. If you find some, add these in the blank spaces provided, giving each a "1" to "5" rating as well.

Another method of reviewing and analyzing your stress is to identify the general pattern or factor into which your stressors fall. Table 2.1 gives four administrative stress sources into which the items in Exercise 2.2 can be placed. The first source, *role-based stress*, is perceived from the principal's role-set interactions and beliefs or attitudes about his or her role in the schools. The second source, *task-based stress*, arises from the performance of day-to-day administrative activities, from telephone and staff interruptions, meetings, writing memos and reports to participating in school activities outside the normal working hours. The third source, *boundary-spanning stress*, emanates from external conditions, such as negotiations and gaining public support for school budgets. The fourth source, *conflict-mediating stress*, arises from the administrator's handling conflicts within the school, such as trying to resolve differences between and among students, resolving parents and school conflicts, and handling student discipline problems.

Can you draw any conclusions from the sources of stress that characterize your work? For comparative purposes the following section summarizes some of the top stress traps of principals, from the elementary to the secondary levels of administration.

Stress Traps of Elementary to Secondary Principals

It would not be difficult to agree that while the principalship is generic in many ways, principals at the elementary and secondary levels probably experience different kinds of stressors. A recent study of 1,000 administrators identified the top 10 stressors for each level of the principalship (Torelli & Gmelch, 1993). The top stressors and percent of principals who indicated high or severe stress ("4" or "5" on the 5-point stress ratings) on each item are indicated in Tables 2.2, 2.3, and 2.4.

Exercise 2.2

Administrative Stress Index

School administrators have identified the following 35 work-related situations as sources of concern. It's possible that some of these situations bother you more than others. How much are you bothered by each of the situations listed below? Please circle the appropriate response.

	Bothers me				
	Rarely				Frequently
1. Being interrupted frequently by telephone calls	1	2	3	4	5
2. Supervising and coordinating the tasks of many people	1	2	3	4	5
3. Feeling staff members don't understand my goals and expectations	1	2	3	4	5
4. Feeling that I am not fully qualified to handle my job	1	2	3	4	5
5. Knowing I can't get information needed to carry out my job properly	1	2	3	4	5
6. Thinking that I will not be able to satisfy the conflicting demands of those who have authority over me	1	2	3	4	5
7. Trying to resolve differences between/among students	1	2	3	4	5
8. Feeling not enough is expected of me by my superiors	1	2	3	4	5
9. Having my work frequently interrupted by staff members who want to talk	1	2	3	4	5
10. Imposing excessively high expectations on myself	1	2	3	4	5
11. Feeling pressure for better job performance over and above what I think is reasonable	1	2	3	4	5
12. Writing memos, letters, and other communications	1	2	3	4	5
13. Trying to resolve differences with my supervisors	1	2	3	4	5
14. Speaking in front of groups	1	2	3	4	5
15. Attempting to meet social expectations (service clubs, friends, and the like)	1	2	3	4	5
16. Not knowing what my supervisor thinks of me, or how he/she evaluates my performance	1	2	3	4	5

(continued)

Exercise 2.2 Continued

	Bothers me				
	Rarely				Frequently
	1	2	3	4	5
17. Having to make decisions that affect the lives of others (colleagues, staff members, students)	1	2	3	4	5
18. Feeling I have to participate in school activities at the expense of my personal time	1	2	3	4	5
19. Feeling that I have too much responsibility delegated to me by my supervisors	1	2	3	4	5
20. Trying to resolve parent/school conflicts	1	2	3	4	5
21. Preparing and allocating budget resources	1	2	3	4	5
22. Feeling that I have too little authority to carry out responsibilities assigned to me	1	2	3	4	5
23. Handling student discipline problems	1	2	3	4	5
24. Being involved in the collective bargaining process	1	2	3	4	5
25. Evaluating staff members' performance	1	2	3	4	5
26. Feeling that I have too heavy a workload, one that I cannot possibly finish during the normal work day	1	2	3	4	5
27. Complying with state, federal, and organizational rules and policies	1	2	3	4	5
28. Feeling that my progress on the job is not what it should or could be	1	2	3	4	5
29. Administering the negotiated contract (grievances, interpretations, and so on)	1	2	3	4	5
30. Being unclear on just what the scope and responsibilities of my job are	1	2	3	4	5
31. Feeling that meetings take up too much time	1	2	3	4	5
32. Trying to complete reports and other paperwork on time	1	2	3	4	5
33. Trying to resolve differences between/among staff members	1	2	3	4	5
34. Trying to influence my immediate supervisor's actions and decisions that affect me	1	2	3	4	5
35. Trying to gain public approval and/or financial support for school program	1	2	3	4	5

TABLE 2.1 Administrator Stress Sources

Source 1: Role-Based Stress
1. Knowing I can't get information needed to carry out my job properly
2. Thinking that I will not be able to satisfy the conflicting demands of those who have authority over me
3. Trying to resolve differences with my superiors
4. Not knowing what my superior thinks of me or how he/she evaluates my performance
5. Feeling that I have too little authority to carry out responsibilities assigned to me
6. Being unclear on just what the scope and responsibilities of my job are
7. Trying to influence my immediate supervisor's actions and decisions that affect me

Source 2: Task-Based Stress
8. Being interrupted frequently by telephone calls
9. Supervising and coordinating the tasks of many people
10. Having my work frequently interrupted by staff members who want to talk
11. Imposing excessively high expectations on myself
12. Writing memos, letters, and other communications
13. Feeling I have to participate in school activities outside of the normal working hours at the expense of my personal time
14. Feeling I have too much responsibility delegated to me by my superior
15. Feeling that I have too heavy a workload, one that I cannot possibly finish during the normal workday
16. Feeling that meetings take up too much time
17. Trying to complete reports and other paperwork on time

Source 3: Boundary-Spanning Stress
18. Preparing and allocating budget resources
19. Being involved in the collective bargaining process
20. Complying with state, federal, and organizational rules and policies
21. Administering the negotiated contract (grievances, interpretations, and so on)
22. Trying to gain public approval and/or financial support for school programs

(*continued*)

TABLE 2.1 Continued

Source 4: Conflict-Mediating Stress
23. Trying to resolve differences between/among students
24. Trying to resolve parent/school conflicts
25. Handling student discipline problems
26. Evaluating staff members' performance
27. Trying to resolve differences between/among staff
28. Having to make decisions affecting the lives of others

TABLE 2.2 Elementary Principals' Top 10 Stressors

1. Too heavy a workload, one that I cannot possibly finish during the school day	46%
2. Meetings take up too much time	43%
3. Completing reports/paperwork on time	40%
4. Can't get information to properly carry out my job	39%
5. Participating in school activities at expense of personal time	37%
6. Progress of my job not what it should/could be	37%
7. Imposing excessively high self-expectations	36%
8. Resolving parent/school conflicts	31%
9. Making decisions that affect lives of others	27%
10. Gaining public support for school programs	27%

A comparative review of Tables 2.2, 2.3, and 2.4 reveals that all three levels of principals share many common stressors. What plagues high school principals, therefore, similarly plagues other members of the principal team. Because you share common problems, the entire team can work together to help each other reduce the barriers to effective school leadership.

You may also wish to look for patterns of stress sources among your leadership team. Categorically, elementary principals reported more significant task-based stress than did their counterparts at the secondary level. One explanation could be the more routine and/or boring tasks they engage in during their workday. Additionally, elementary principals are usually the only administrator in the building, thus lacking support or sharing of the administrative load

TABLE 2.3 Middle School/Junior High Principals' Top 10 Stressors

1. Meetings take up too much time	45%
2. Imposing excessively high self-expectations	43%
3. Too heavy a workload, one I cannot finish during the school day	42%
4. Can't get information to carry out my job	40%
5. Progress of my job not what it should/could be	36%
6. Completing reports/paperwork on time	34%
7. Resolving parent/school conflicts	32%
8. Not being able to satisfy conflicting demands of supervisors	27%
9. Participating in school activities at the expense of personal time	27%
10. Gaining public support for school programs	27%

TABLE 2.4 High School Principals' Top 10 Stressors

1. Participating in school activities at the expense of personal time	46%
2. Meetings take up too much time	44%
3. Can't get information to carry out my job	43%
4. Imposing excessively high self-expectations	39%
5. Too heavy a workload, one I cannot finish during the school day	37%
6. Progress of my job not what it should/could be	34%
7. Completing reports/paperwork on time	29%
8. Resolving parent/school conflicts	27%
9. Not able to satisfy conflicting demands of my supervisors	25%
10. Meeting social expectations	25%

by assistant principals. The greater isolation created by being the singular building administrator may lead elementary principals to perceive high levels of work overload, task difficulty, and the need for increased achievement.

Conflict-mediating stress was also significantly greater within the elementary principals, decreased from elementary to middle school to high school, and was less significant in the superintendency. As the sole mediator within the elementary building, the perception is that the elementary principal is the only conduit for the resolution of all conflicts, ranging from student-student to administrator-teacher. Many more conflicts at the secondary level, specifically student-student and parent-school, are typically handled within the classroom teacher's arena, thus effectively eliminating a whole host of irons from the principal's administrative fire.

What does all this mean to the building principal? What are the traps inherent within the principalship? Understanding the dangers and arenas of risk, what can a principal do to transcend the anxieties and win the battle over stress and its resultant denigration of performance? How do principals operate on a daily basis to move from a stress-laden, negatively affected performance to a positive and effective performance? How do they achieve a performance honed to a cutting edge by the engine of stress—that is, maintaining peak performance with full utilization of stress as a component?

Too often administrators allow the nature of stress to push the individual to a level of denigrated performance, commonly referred to as burnout. We can see its results through symbolic behaviors of colleagues dwelling within this area of their performance curve. Signals include lackluster interest in their work, increased illnesses, lack of decision-making initiative, irrational problem solving, easy level of exhaustion, and low self-esteem.

The vicious cycle of the stress trap experienced by many administrators can be easily described. Typically, a high school principal believes that active involvement in the school's activities outside the normal working hours can and will lead to a more successful principalship. It is not uncommon for high school principals to be engaged in evening and after-school activities 3 or 4 nights out of the week. This "extra" attention supersedes the time available for the principal to complete the daily tasks that face all school administrators. Because of the decreased availability of time as a resource, most principals believe that they must take more of their personal time just to finish the reports and paperwork associated with operating a school. The increased commitment and the shift of personal time to the professional role thus effectively supplant an entire segment of the individual's being, that is, room for individual and personal tasks and growth. Feeling that putting more time into the job only seems to set the administrator further and further back sets up the conditions for feelings of incompetence and the demise of personal self-esteem. Suddenly, principals' tasks appear insurmountable and as immense as a tidal wave, with no easily defined escape.

The trap has been set for this unfortunate high school principal. The faster the principal runs, the faster the treadmill spins under-foot—often causing the principal to fall off.

Stress and Gender: The Androgynous Principal

Some researchers believe that masculinity and femininity are com-plementary, not opposite, domains of trait and behavior (Ben, 1981). An administrator of either sex may be both masculine and feminine and thus be androgynous (a combination of the Greek *andro* for male and *gyn* for female). Men and women principals should be both sensi-tive and tough, strong and gentle, emotional and rational, and so on. Thus androgyny means combining male and female behaviors, which allow you to act as individuals rather than stereotypes, to express and embrace all aspects of your personalities.

"Freeing the slaves frees the master." Many administrators have become slaves of male and female behaviors without the freedom to call upon the full repertoire of human behavior available to all individuals. Researchers also believe that besides freeing themselves from stereotypes, androgynous people are more adaptable, flexible in their behavior patterns, and clever in problem solving. Further-more, androgynous individuals are in command of basic facts, have balanced learning habits, are quick thinking and creative, and pos-sess social skills (Sargent, 1981).

Administrators in our study who were classified as androgynous had significantly less stress and burnout than those who were classified as either just masculine or just feminine. They had signifi-cantly lower role-based stress, boundary-spanning stress, emotional exhaustion, and depersonalization. Androgynous administrators also had significantly higher mean scores on personal accomplish-ments. The association of sex-role orientation with stress and burnout tends to suggest that androgynous administrators perceive them-selves as having less stress and lower frequency of burnout.

The Principal-Secretary Team

No school can be effective without considering the most integral element in any principal's performance—the secretary-principal team. International management consultant R. Alec Mackenzie (1990) contends that of the many resources contributing to the manager's effectiveness, none is more critical than his or her secretary. It is imperative then, that you and your secretary work together to reduce each other's stress.

A study of more than 200 school secretaries reveals their major sources of stress:

1. Being interrupted frequently by telephone calls and drop-in visitors
2. Waiting to get information needed to carry out my job
3. Imposing excessively high expectations on myself
4. Feeling that I have too heavy a workload, one that I cannot possibly finish during the normal workday
5. Feeling that I have too little authority to carry out responsibilities assigned to me
6. Being treated as less important by professional staff
7. Working in a noisy, disruptive environment
8. Needing to see my principal and not being able to
9. Trying to get the principal to complete reports and other paperwork on time
10. Being bored by routine tasks

Both you and your secretary must work together to solve common stresses that plague you in the office. The Secretarial Stress Index and Secretary-Principal Stressors Profile in the Appendix will help you identify common stressors you may wish to work on together.

Chapter 3 will take you through the next steps to assist you in the selection and resolution of your most bothersome stress traps.

3

Principals Taking Action

The previous chapters provided the background and information necessary to begin a comprehensive administrative stress reduction program. Like so many administrators, you may have gone directly to this chapter, omitting the others because you need immediate answers to your particular problems. If this is the case, we strongly recommend that you go back and read the previous chapters. The basics must be understood before lasting solutions can be selected.

Also, before you begin this chapter consider its basic assumption: Most principal stressors can be controlled and should be attacked at the cause level. Good executives learn to manage the causes of problems, not just mask their symptoms. While aspirin provides temporary relief, managing stressors produces permanent results. Before you take the quickest and easiest path to reduce your tension, try the Principal Action Plan. It will help you successfully reduce your stress by controlling your problems rather than having them control you.

The Goal of the Principal Action Plan

When you use the Principal Action Plan, your main goal will be to first identify and then reconstruct your personal stressors. In doing this, you will analyze the causes of each stressor, examine potential solutions, and finally take corrective actions. When you have finished this chapter, you should be able to develop and implement your own program without the aid of machines, technicians, or medical devices. Ultimately, this will result in a decrease in your stress level.

Each step is part of a sequence of activities that will help you go from being controlled by your stressor to being in control of it. The steps are:

1. Identify your most bothersome stressors and select one to resolve.
2. Search for the causes of this stressful event.
3. Generate a set of possible solutions to remedy the causes.
4. Specify a plan of action you will take to alleviate one cause.
5. Develop a timetable to implement your plan of action.
6. Set a date and method for how you will follow up and evaluate the effectiveness of your plan.
7. Investigate the potential problems or unintended consequences (additional stress) your action plan may have created.

A principal who not only understands the stress principles and concepts presented in the previous chapters but can also apply the above set of strategies to his or her stress problems will gain several advantages. First, since the plan is segmented into seven parts—each an integral sequence in the overall process—you will always know where you are and what has to be done. Second, when you adopt this plan as part of your managerial problem-solving style, you will then have a framework to guide you in processing information to resolve future managerial and personal crises. Third, such a process can easily be explained to your faculty and staff and can thus assist them in their stress reduction efforts. Finally, whereas any single quick and easy stress remedy may be applicable to only a few, this process can help all principals control their stress.

Nevertheless, the plan has one major weakness. You may find yourself avoiding the seven steps because the process seems too systematic, too rigidly mechanical. True, it is systematic; that is what makes it work so well. It presupposes that administrators have the organizational skills and foresight to put a program into action and see it through to its completion.

Conditions for Success: The CASH Formula

The effectiveness of the plan depends on the fulfillment of four conditions. These conditions are represented by the acronym CASH, signifying the payoff you can expect by having the right amount of Control over your job, facilitating an Attitude of commitment, an openness to learn new Skills, and the dedication to develop the skills into helpful Habits. Let us look at each of these conditions to understand how CASH can provide the mental and physical relief from burdensome debits of stress.

1: Control

Principals under stress often believe that they are out of control, that they cannot change the circumstances causing them stress. However, the changes needed to overcome stress many times do lie within your powers. You can change and influence your own behaviors and, to some extent, the conditions of your job. This is a basic assumption that must be held in order to progress any further with the stress program.

Pressures can be avoided by shifting from being controlled by one's job to being in control of it. While all principals have the ultimate choice of alleviating stress by quitting their jobs, we hope the driving force of stress does not lead to this end. Somewhere in between burning out and dropping out lies an area of influence where principals can exert some discretionary control and cope with the pressures.

Remember, of course, our goal is neither to rid ourselves of all tension nor to control it. Some stress goads us to success and, with the aid of a systematic stress program, can become a friend rather than a foe of the effective administrator.

2: Attitude

The next critical ingredient to "cashing" in on the stress plan rests with having the right attitude, the commitment to making it happen.

The first commitment takes the form of a set time to learn some new skills and habits, to begin the action plan. Do you have the time and energy? If so, block off some uninterruptible time on your daily calendar to begin your plan. Preferably take a couple of hours in the early morning in your office on a predictably slow day. Have your secretary protect your time by screening all calls and visitors.

Now that you have your time blocked off for undivided attention, you must commit your energy to produce effective responses to the seven steps of the process. If some unforeseen crisis arises and robs you of your private time, reschedule another appointment with yourself, just as you would for an important visitor. Also remember that once you have begun your plan, you must resist demands that might disrupt your execution time.

One method that some principals find helpful in fulfilling their commitments is instituting a contract—something all administrators should understand and respect. *Contract* in this sense means making an agreement with yourself to complete the seven-step plan by putting it in writing. Table 3.1 represents a sample contract. Notice the option for enlisting the help of your secretary or one of your colleagues.

3: Skill

Now that you have the commitment, you must develop the skills needed to fulfill your plan. Skill building represents another characteristic of successful principals. The ability to grow with the job and its new challenges is the essence of effective coping behavior.

The notion that good educators are born, not made, must be dispelled and replaced with the opposite truism. New skills can give desperate administrators new ways of controlling their actions, feelings, and behaviors. In fact, if we assume people learned the counterproductive behaviors that now cause them stress, reducing stress is merely a matter of substituting those unproductive behaviors with new skills conducive to coping.

TABLE 3.1 A Self-Contract Principal Action Stress Program

I, _____ , hereby commit my time and energy to completing the Principal Action Plan for Stress. During the next month, I will schedule the following times each day to develop, execute, and evaluate my progress toward completion of the program.

Activity Monitor

Date:

	Scheduled	Completed
7:00		
7:30		
8:00		
8:30		
9:00		
9:30		
10:00		
10:30		
11:00		
11:30		
12:00		
12:30		
1:00		
1:30		
2:00		
2:30		
3:00		
3:30		
4:00		
4:30		
5:00		
5:30		
6:00		
6:30		

Granted, this is easier stated than started. Nevertheless, the purpose of this chapter is to provide you with the framework and system to do just that.

4: Habit

Learning the skills to reduce stress is not enough. The many managerial self-help books and on-the-job training seminars available today provide most principals with the ability to distinguish effective from ineffective practices. However, the impact of both is usually short-lived. This knowledge must be formulated into a plan of action and implemented before any meaningful change can take place. Skills have to be practiced until they become part of one's routine or behavior before they can produce any appreciable change in performance.

For instance, consider the controversial "open door policy," which states that principals must be continually accessible to teachers, staff, and others. We know it is also a perennial promoter of interruptions, one of the most significant stressors affecting administrators. A simple skill to screen interruptions would be to selectively close your door for uninterrupted planning time. While the skill is simple, the process of making it a habit becomes very difficult. How did you feel the first time you closed your office door to allow yourself time in your office alone? If you were like most, you became anxious, nervous, and uncomfortable. With the door open, you could hear what was going on outside your office, but now the closed door represents isolation from outside interests. As a result, you begin to respond negatively and before you know it, you've interrupted yourself by emerging from your office for a self-imposed break.

Administrators who have gone through time management training know the positive effect a reasonable "closed door" skill can have on their effectiveness. But the old habit feels more comfortable and thus prevails. This is the exact same dilemma you will face when attempting to behave differently, based on your stress plan. We can predict that you will feel more comfortable using your old style, but you must resist this temptation in order to build the habits that make a successful stress reduction program.

A Word of Caution

Even if you have all four components in the CASH formula working for you, you may still encounter difficulties. If you initially choose a stressor that is too cumbersome, move to an easier stressor. Also, you may wish to seek assistance in diagnosing and solving the stressful situation. It is best to select a stressor over which you have more control and a greater chance of success. But if you need help, do not hesitate to ask for assistance, because what bothers you most likely stresses your colleagues as well. Two key resources are your administrative team and your secretary, both of whom would probably welcome the opportunity to resolve common office stressors affecting all of you.

Now that you have the CASH to begin the stress program, start with Step 1 and proceed sequentially through Step 7.

Step 1—Stressor Selection: Where Should I Start?

The objective of this first step is to select a stressor you wish to resolve. As a beginning, the Administrative Stress Index in the previous chapter gives you a list of potential problems to pursue. List the top 10 most bothersome stressors from this index in Exercise 3.1.

To this list add any other major problems you have currently identified as unique to your position, school, and/or district. Consider other experiences you have recently encountered. You should now have between 10 and 15 problem areas from which to select one to work on through the duration of the seven-step plan in this chapter.

The next question is where to begin. Before making your decision, consider three criteria useful in making your selection. First, reconsider the issue of control. You will recall that in the last section you were asked whether each of the stressors was internally controlled and managed by you, or externally induced and beyond your control. Read down the list of stressors and put a check in the "control" column next to each stressor if you feel you can personally change it.

For example, principals view their influence over rules and regulations as minimal at the national and state level but stronger within their own district and school. However, they see their ability to control

Exercise 3.1

Stressor Selection

---

1. List below your top 10 stressors identified from the Administrative Stress Index in Chapter 2.
2. Add three to five other stressors you have recently encountered.
3. Read down your list of stressors and check Column 1 if you feel you have control over this stressor, and explain why.
4. For each stressor over which you have indicated control, check Column 2 if you also believe your efforts to change it will be successful, and explain why.
5. Finally, for those stressors for which you have indicated both control and success, check Column 3 if you believe resolving this problem is important to your effective performance, and comment.

Stressor		Control		Success		Importance
1.						
2.						
3.						
4.						
5.						
6.						
7.						
8.						
9.						
10.						
11.						
12.						
13.						
14.						
15.						

Write below the stressor you have selected that meets all three criteria of control, success, and importance.

---

the quality and quantity of meetings more optimistically. At first glance you may say, "I can't control what goes on in meetings, nor can I dictate how many I'm scheduled to attend." But aren't some meetings within your realm of control, at least the ones you call to order? Consider similarly each stressor on your list, indicate whether you can control it, and state the rationale for your decision.

Next consider the issue of success. Not only is it critical that you have control over your stressor, but being successful in your first stress program is equally important. Your successes will reinforce your confidence and commit you to continue resolving more difficult stressors as they arise. For those stressors for which you have indicated possible control, ask this second question: If I attempt to resolve this stressor, am I likely to succeed? Place your answer in the second column and again provide a rationale for your decision. If you feel that success with "meetings" is dependent upon the cooperation of your staff and faculty, then set this problem aside until you can enlist their assistance. On the other hand, you may feel "too heavy a workload" is within your control and can be successfully reduced. Most principals might agree, since much of their overwork stems from workaholic attitudes and unwillingness to give up responsibility, both factors they can do something about.

By now you should have five to eight stressors that have met the first two criteria. Last, determine how important resolving these stressors is to your effective performance. Do not necessarily equate importance with urgency. Think more in terms of present barriers you need to remove in order to continue being a productive educator. Record your answer to this criterion in the third column and again write down the basis for your decision.

A few critical stressors should now have emerged, meeting all three criteria: under your control, with the possibility of success, and of importance to your job. Select one of these remaining few and write it at the bottom of the form in Exercise 3.1. If nothing stands out as being more critical than others, then select the one which, if resolved, will also reduce the stress of others in your school. In this way you can act as a stress reliever for yourself and at the same time a stress filter for your staff.

TABLE 3.2 The Case of the "Heavy Workload"

Clues (Sources)	Culprits (Causes)	Consequences (Effects)
1. Environmental	overcrowded working conditions drop-in visitors open-office concept	Backaches Headaches
2. Organizational	unclear job responsi-bilities unfair work distri-bution seasonal work backlog	Insomnia Heart Disease
3. Interpersonal	unwillingness to confront others thinking others can perform unable to motivate others	Ulcers Cancer
4. Personal	inability to say no unrealistic appraisal of time unproductive use of time	Nervousness Neurosis
5. External	incomplete avocational interest overcommitted to serve community pressure from family and friends	Hypertension Skin Disorder

Step 2—Causes: How Did I Get It?

Failure to resolve stressors stems from one basic fact: The cause has not been discovered. Everything, from a menacing cough to a mental collapse, has a cause. To rid yourself of these malignant effects, you must first know how they came to be.

Think of the search for causes in terms of detective work. For instance, Table 3.2 lays out "the case of the heavy workload." We are already familiar with the consequences of this mystery—headaches, backaches, ulcers, insomnia, and sometimes death. Our task now is to do some sleuthing—what created the overload?

Begin by looking for clues in the most obvious places. Four sources provide our possible clues: *environmental* conditions (overcrowding, excessive noise, heat, and cold); *organizational* factors (role conflict, job ambiguity, and managing people); *interpersonal* influences (personality conflicts, mistrust, lack of support, and overcompetitiveness); and *personal* propensities (driving too hard, unrelenting pace, and being hyperalert). To these sources add other significant pressures *external* to your work activities, including demands for time and attention from family, friends, recreation, hobbies, and other interests outside the realm of the working world.

Within each of these sources lie potential causes. Unlike simple problems, stressors result from a multitude of causes. Much as in the case of Agatha Christie's thriller *Murder on the Orient Express*, the detective must dismiss the simple single-murderer solution as too obvious and then find as many as a dozen culprits who also contribute equally to the crime. Recognizing that a stressor may have multiple causes and may originate from several sources, let us see if we can disclose the suspects in the "heavy workload" case. Listed on page 48 are a few clues from each source. Can you add any others?

Now turn your attention to the stressor you selected in Step 1. Write it out in section A of Exercise 3.2. In section B list all the possible causes of your stressful event. To the right of each of the causes indicate its source: either personal, external, environmental, organizational, or interpersonal.

Step 3—Solutions: What Can I Do About It?

The solution step generates alternatives that will alleviate the causes you have identified in Step 2. But you must do Steps 1 and 2 first. To go right to solutions without first exploring the causes may lead you in the wrong direction or to the wrong conclusion.

Generating alternatives is not a haphazard activity, but a logical, thoughtful, and careful search for specific actions that will alleviate the cause. Use the causes identified in Exercise 3.2 as a set of problem

Exercise 3.2

Identification of Causes

Section A: From Exercise 3.1, write below the stressor you want to
resolve.

_____

_____

Section B: List as many causes of the above stressor as possible,
indicating to the right the source of the cause (Environmental, Organizational, Interpersonal, Personal, or
External).

	Causes	Sources
1.		
2.		
3.		
4.		
5.		

---

statements from which to develop your solutions. Begin by trans-
ferring the causes from Exercise 3.2 to Exercise 3.3.

Next you will identify solutions for each cause. Let's explore this.
To come up with sound solutions, you need to not only logically
draw from your past experiences and your knowledge of management practices but also creatively look forward for innovative ideas
suitable to your situation. For example, to attack the cause of "unrealistic appraisal of time it takes to complete tasks," a logical solution would be to first keep a personal time log to audit how and
where your time is presently spent. It may be helpful to refer to
Mackenzie's *The Time Trap* (1990) for useful time log techniques.

Principals have always been trained in and rewarded for their
logical thinking. Now is the time to nurture your creative thought
process. Since many management tools may not be applicable in
resolving some common causes of stress, you may have to create

Exercise 3.3

Generating Solutions

Instructions:

1. Relist the causes you identified in Exercise 3.2 in the column marked "causes" below.

2. To the right of each cause, identify a solution that will attack the problem.

                        Causes   Solutions

1. _____

2. _____

3. _____

4. _____

5. _____

---

new solutions to fit your specific work situations. Basically, you have four reservoirs of creative solutions available to you. First, consult other people in your school district. One idea tends to generate others, and the more viewpoints you can gather, the better the set of alternatives you will have to select from. Second, check with consultants or third parties who have the advantage of being distant enough to see what we cannot see ourselves. All too often the solution is right under our noses, hence out of sight. Third, refer to the volumes of self-help books readily available in today's bookstores. Although all do not provide sound judgment, use your own common sense to glean the good from the trash. Finally, search your own subconscious for innovative ideas. Our logical, domineering left side of the brain sometimes acts as a constraint to creative thinking. Many techniques are available to help you reactivate a more balanced search for solutions.

Across from the causes listed in Exercise 3.3, fill in your solutions. Whatever you do, just keep thinking. As Samuel Johnson concluded, "There isn't a problem the human mind can devise that the human mind cannot also solve."

Step 4—Plan of Action:
What Solution Best Resolves the Stress?

Now you are ready to take action. But let us first briefly review what you have accomplished so far. In Step 1 you selected a stressor as your target for alleviation. Step 2 generated a list of causes, followed by Step 3, which identified solutions to each of the causes.

Review your set of solutions and select one solution as a plan that suits you best. Your choice should not be taken lightly and left to chance. Consider a definite strategy upon which to select your plan. First, be wise and start with a small, modest, and manageable solution. No step or plan of action is too small. A grandiose, unrealistic, and over-perfectionistic plan may be discouraging and lead you to total abandonment in the long run. Adopt a one-step-at-a-time strategy of change.

Second, your first plan should be chosen on the basis of creating the least change and disruption to your routine and organizational flow. While at first this may seem contrary and counterproductive to achieving great gains, remember that with change comes stress, too. Too much change, we have discovered, may cause too much disruption and resistance to your plan. Therefore, select the plan that has the greatest potential for being unobtrusive (but still productive) to your general managerial style.

Third, choose a plan that assures you success the first time around. Your success will reinforce your confidence and increase your effectiveness in implementing more difficult changes in the future.

Finally, and most important, work on one plan at a time. If you attempt too much by juggling several plans simultaneously, you may become confused and discouraged and eventually end up more stressed than ever.

Now, select your plan of action from the list of solutions you generated previously and write out your plan in section A of Exercise 3.4. Remember to make your decision based on a gradual, unobtrusive, successful, and singular approach.

What impact do you feel your plan will have on reducing or alleviating your stress? Typically, plans of action can be categorized into any one of five tension-reducing actions.

1. Interim action—usually the first kind of action taken to keep you going while you are still searching for the long-term solution to the cause.
2. Adaptive action—appropriate when you find out that the causes are unresolvable and unremovable. You then revert to minimizing the effects of the cause, since it usually lies outside your influence or control.
3. Corrective action—eliminates the cause that produced the stress in the first place. This is what all administrators desire; the most efficient and effective course of action.
4. Preventive action—removes the possible cause of the stressor, or its probability of occurring before it attacks. Such action is typically known in the world of health as preventive medicine or high-level wellness.
5. Contingent action—provides stand-by actions to offset or minimize the effects of a serious attack. The administrator decides which actions will keep possible causes from occurring. Some engineers refer to this as contingency planning.

The first three actions (interim, adaptive, and corrective) play a major role in the Principal Action Plan. The last two, however, define what principals can do to alleviate stress before it arises.

The importance of recognizing the differences in the capabilities and purposes among the first three kinds of action cannot be emphasized enough. Without recognizing the strengths and limitations of each, you may find yourself believing you have corrected the cause when you have really only adapted to the tension level. Therefore, complete Exercise 3.4 by identifying the type of plan you have selected. Is it corrective, adaptive, or interim? If it is adaptive or interim, have you also planned to reattack the cause later with a truly corrective action?

If you plan to alleviate rather than just temporarily reduce your tension level, you should make that commitment now as a footnote to your action plan.

Exercise 3.4

Developing a Plan of Action

Instructions:
1. Review your set of solutions in Exercise 3.3, select one, and write it out as a plan of action in section A.
2. In section B, indicate whether your plan is corrective, interim, or adaptive and give both the strengths and weaknesses of your plan.
3. If your plan is adaptive or interim, is there anything you can do to reattack the cause at a later date? If so, note your intentions in section C.

Section A: My Plan of Action is to:

_____

_____

Section B: My Plan is primarily: __ Corrective   __ Preventive
                                     __ Interim   __ Contingent
                                     __ Adaptive   __ Other

Its major strengths are:
1. _____
2. _____
3. _____

Its major weaknesses are:
1. _____
2. _____
3. _____

(Optional)
Section C: I plan to reattack the cause by:

_____

_____

Step 5—Implementation: How, When, and Where Should I Start My Plan?

Now you have identified the causes of stress, suggested solutions, and decided on a plan of action. Your next task is to learn to integrate your plan into your everyday managerial style. It is much like learning to play a game of golf. If, for instance, you want to be an all-around golfer, you have to develop the ability to perform each required skill successfully. Playing a complete game of golf depends not only on learning the basics of how to drive, chip, and putt, but also avoiding water hazards and blasting out of sand traps.

Merely reading books or making mental pictures does not produce great golfers; it takes practice to perfect skills. Similarly, you learn how to manage hazards and traps by analyzing the situation, taking practice swings, compensating for conditions beyond your control, and finally standing up there and blasting your way out.

Everything you have done to this point leads to this critical step. Now is your time to put your new plan into action. In Exercise 3.5 you first restate what you will be doing (e.g., prioritizing my tasks each day into high-payoff and low-payoff activities); where (e.g., in my office); and how often and when (e.g., first thing in the morning at 7 a.m.). Finally, do it. Stop analyzing, planning, and proliferating and start producing, for "today is the first day of the rest of your life."

Step 6—Evaluation: How Will I Know if It Worked?

Any plan should contain steps to review and assess your progress, followed by modification of the action if it produced unwanted results. This is the purpose of Steps 6 and 7. The follow-up evaluation alerts you as to whether the plan you set in motion actually created the desired results. In other words, has your plan been carried out? Have you developed some proficiency in the new skill area?

To check whether you have followed through, take out your daily appointment book and see if you have kept your appointments to practice your skill at the time and place you specified in the implemen-

Exercise 3.5

Implementing Your Plan

Instructions:
Indicate below the activities you will use to fulfill your plan, where you will conduct them, how often, and when they will be completed.

	Activities	Where	How Often	When
1.				
2.				
3.				
4.				
5.				
6.				
7.				
8.				
9.				
10.				

---

tation phase. If your plan was to prioritize your tasks every morning before engaging in your daily routine, check to see how proficiently and diligently you have adhered to your plan.

On the other hand, if your plan has not worked out as originally scheduled, be flexible and reset your path. You may have set unrealistic expectations for yourself that now have to be readjusted.

Next, you will want to know if this skill has now become internalized. If so, has it helped reduce your stress? A word of caution is in order here: Don't expect too much. First, review your plan to see if it was a corrective, interim, or adaptive course of action. If it was corrective, your goal should have been to alleviate the cause. Interim and adaptive actions are more limited and should be expected to reduce the cause only until corrective action can be taken.

Exercise 3.6

Follow-Up Evaluation

---

1. By what means did you check to see if your plan was successfully implemented?

   _____

   _____

2. Was your plan fully implemented?   __ Yes   __ No
   If not, why? _____

3. What results were obtained?

   _____

   _____

4. Can your plan be modified to give you better results?
   __ Yes   __No
   If so, how? _____

   _____

Summarize your evaluation of your actions in Exercise 3.6. Again, do not expect too much from your first plan of action. Be willing to modify your action and, if need be, set your sights a bit lower for now.

Step 7—Unintended Consequences: What Additional Stress Have I Caused?

As has been stated before, any change by itself will be stressful. Your plan has most likely changed your behavior and the way you interact both with your staff and the organization as a whole. Therefore, regardless of whether your plan has been successful, it has had some impact on other elements critical to you and your organization's effectiveness.

Assess what additional stress and strain you may have caused the organization due to your new plan of action. Write these below in Exercise 3.7. Some promising places you might look for these side

Exercise 3.7

Assessing the Impact

A. What additional benefits did you receive from your plan that you had not expected?

1. _____

2. _____

3. _____

4. _____

5. _____

B. Besides the benefits, what were some unintended negative consequences or additional strains your plan created?

1. _____

2. _____

3. _____

4. _____

5. _____

C. Should any of these negative consequences be alleviated?

___ Yes   ___No

D. If so, in what ways could your plan be modified to rectify the unwanted consequences?

1. _____

2. _____

3. _____

4. _____

5. _____

E. Go back and modify your Plan of Action and Implementing Your Plan documents accordingly.

---

effects are in your own performance, the generation of ideas, effectiveness of group processes, influences on others, and expenditure of time, material, and money.

For example, was your goal to reduce your present workload, and your course of action to prioritize your tasks into high- and low-payoff activities? If so, your plan should have reduced some of the pressures and overcommitments in your job. However, in place of the time taken for attending to low-payoff tasks, you may have accepted additional responsibilities. Delegating these low-payoff items to your staff may have also caused a slowdown in their productivity. In other words, you may have accomplished the intended action of your plan, but in the meantime have incurred additional costs along with the intended benefits. These undesirable and unwanted results are what you might refer to as negative unintended consequences.

Ask yourself if these consequences should also be alleviated and rectified. If so, make modifications in your plan to reduce these unwanted side effects.

Concluding Comments

Once you have mastered and fully understand each of the seven steps in the stress reduction program, all seven components can easily be condensed and summarized into one useful worksheet. For example, the seven-step worksheet shown in Table 3.3 represents a summarization of the stressor "too heavy a workload."

It is now time to use this worksheet in developing your next stress reduction plan. Remember that the first and all subsequent plans must be maintained in order to sustain your progress. This process is incremental and synergetic; one plan builds on another and another, resulting in the development of a managerial wellness profile. As each skill becomes a habit and part of your repertoire of coping techniques, be sure to maintain these skills so you don't regress or fall back on old unhealthy habits. As Mark Twain once remarked, "Quitting smoking is easy; I've done it hundreds of times." Make sure any stress you have taken off, stays off.

TABLE 3.3 Principal Action Plan

I. Most Bothersome Stress Event: Too heavy a workload, one that cannot be finished in a day.

II. Causes	III. Solutions	IV. Specific Action Plan
1. Unrealistic appraisal of time. 2. Inability to say no. 3. Overcommited to work over family and personal time. 4. Unclear delineation of responsibilities. 5. Cannot distinguish between high and low priorities.	1. Conduct time schedules. 2. Gain assertive skills. 3. Set family/job goals. 4. Request specific job description. 5. Concentrate on high-payoff tasks.	a. The plan is to: Concentrate on high-payoff tasks. b. Type of Action: ___ Corrective ___ Interim ___ Preventive ___ Adaptive ___ Contingent ___ Other

V. Steps for Implementation

1. Activity: Develop high-payoff and low-payoff lists
2. Where: In the office at my desk without interruptions
3. How Often: Daily for 2 weeks
4. When: Every morning at 8:30 a.m.

VI. Follow-Up Evaluation

1. Did I write out lists every morning?
2. Were the high-payoff tasks completed first?
3. Did I actually delegate or eliminate any low-payoff tasks?

VII. Negative Unintended Consequences

1. My boss became upset with incomplete tasks.
2. Work became too regimented and not as carefree.
3. I created an overload for my staff by delegating too many tasks.

Modifications of Plans Needed? Since my boss needs to know what I am concentrating on (high payoffs), I should communicate with him/her periodically to seek concurrence with my plan.

4

Principal Stress and Performance

Principal Performance Under Pressure

David Ericson, an inner-city high school principal, used to brag, "I work best when I'm under pressure." His colleagues can remember situations where David would enter faculty meetings poised and ready to respond to anything that came to his attention. He would speak eloquently about each issue, often espousing current research and explaining his personal philosophical agenda for educational change. The pressure that David Ericson spoke of focused on the platform and limelight this charismatic leader sought.

Across town at a neighboring high school was another principal, Robbie Nagasaki. Robbie was also well respected in his community and often asked to speak to civic and parent groups around town. His area of expertise was the cognitive development of adolescents. Robbie's expertise was often sought as a basis for the many decisions his school was facing with respect to the appropriateness of curriculum, inclusive delivery systems, tracking, and grouping infrastructures. Although Robbie's background was extensive and rich, he nevertheless felt intense pressure to guide the staff toward a thoughtful and intelligent decision surrounding each issue. Robbie would typically spend hours researching and preparing his data prior to presenting it to the staff for decision. The staff at Robbie's school believe that each decision made under Robbie's directions and guidance has been a profitable one for both students and school community.

How did David and Robbie differ in the way they responded to pressure? Why do some cope under the same conditions that make others collapse? The answers to these simply stated questions fill volumes of books and journals. The questions perplex many a scientist: Sociologists investigate the dynamics of the work group, psychologists delve into the motives and drives of individuals, ergonomists examine the interaction of the individual and the environment, and anthropologists chronicle the norms, values, and mores of the work culture.

Recently both popular and medical journals have blamed school stress for the ills of principals, from hay fever to heart failure. Some school districts have responded with stress reduction and wellness programs. Others have developed a backlash to the overconcern for stress, saying "If the job's too soft, you lose your mental acuity." At times both sides lose sight of the fact that performance problems in education result from both too much and too little stress. Optimum performance comes from converting tension from an enemy into an ally, from a needless stressor to a creative motivator. Therefore stress becomes an enemy when either too much or too little is produced.

This chapter explores the linkage between stress and effective performance. As researchers have discovered, the effects of stress on performance elude precise measurement. While not easily measured, the link provides the fundamental basis of this book—principal effectiveness. Our goal, therefore, is to search for ways to generate the proper amount of stress for optimum stimulation and performance: first, to stimulate you to become an effective principal, and second, to control stress in order to maintain your effectiveness.

The Competitive Edge

The classic test of this link between stress and performance was conducted on 60 Little League baseball players from four teams over their entire season of 36 games (McGrath, 1976a). The researchers studied the stress of being up at the plate and how well the ball players performed. Each time players stepped up to bat, measures were taken of their level of excitement or arousal (pulse rate, breathing rate, and behavior while in the on-deck circle); batting performance (how well they hit the ball); success at the plate (runners being advanced, runs scored); pressure on the batter (the degree to which the batter's performance would affect the game); criticalness (the potential effect of the game on the team's season success); and the ability of the opposing pitcher (task difficulty).

Two relationships were observed. First the batter's performance was measured against arousal level. As demonstrated in Figure 4.1, a Little Leaguer's batting performance increased in a positive linear fashion as arousal level increased (holding the ability of the opponent constant). The second relationship measured the performance of the batter against the ability of the opposing pitcher—task difficulty—while holding the batter's arousal constant. As might be expected, the batter's performance decreased in a negative linear manner as the opposing pitcher's ability increased (Figure 4.2).

When we combine the effects of arousal (Figure 4.1) and task difficulty (Figure 4.2) on the batter's performance, we find a much different relationship between stress and performance; not a linear one but one that resembles an inverted-U shape (Figure 4.3). That is, at low levels of stress or demand, performance is low because arousal is low. There is not enough stimulation to peak the players' performance; they lose their competitive edge. At high levels of stress, absolute performance is also low, not because arousal is high but in spite of it, because the task difficulty is so high. At moderate amounts of stress, optimum levels of performance are experienced.

Relating the implications of the Little Leaguer study to your job as principal, you can postulate that the effectiveness of job performance depends on three conditions: (1) your state of arousal or stimulation; (2) your talents and capabilities to meet the challenges of leadership; and (3) the difficulty or nature of the workload you

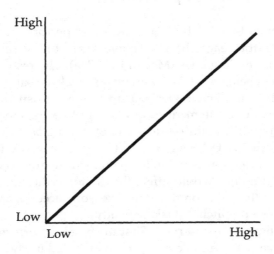

Figure 4.1. Excitement: Performance and Arousal

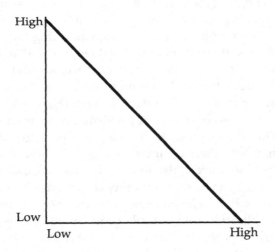

Figure 4.2. Batter's Performance Versus Pitcher's Performance (Task Difficulty)

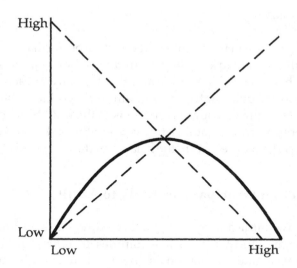

High

Low

Low   High

Figure 4.3. Relationship Between Stress and Performance

have to complete. Let's elaborate a bit on each of these conditions influencing the relationship between stress and performance.

Level of Arousal/Stimulation

What is the relationship between stimulation and stress? As described in Chapter 1, stress is high under both low and high levels of stimulation—under conditions of both distress and eustress. Proper levels of moderate stimulation, therefore, become important in providing productive levels of stress.

Perception of Leadership Ability

The state of arousal or stimulation you experience depends a great deal on your perception of whether you can perform the job well. Can you meet the challenge of the task at hand? This perception depends on both past experiences as an administrator (successes and failures) and the talents you bring into the principal's office.

Nature of Workload

The third condition in the formula for effective performance is the difficulty of the workload you are required to perform, in terms of both the number of tasks to be done and the difficulty of each task. These measures of quantitative and qualitative workload largely depend on how accurate your perception is of the task difficulty, as opposed to your perceived ability to complete the task. The key to optimum job performance rests in the balance of difficulty and ability.

From Principal Disability to Ability

You can draw implications from the three conditions outlined in the Little League study. Take a few minutes to refine and more completely investigate the relationship between stress and your job performance. First, a flow chart in Figure 4.4 explains the relationship among the three conditions (Gmelch, 1983). This chart will then be converted into a stress and performance curve in the next section in this chapter. Finally, the concluding chapters will help you discover how to optimize, maintain, and stabilize your performance in the most productive manner.

Figure 4.4 represents a flow chart on the nature of stress and performance. As was the case with the Little Leaguers, several conditions are important in the performance process. Condition 1.0 represents your perceived ability to successfully complete your work. In other words, do you feel you have the skills and talents to meet the challenges ahead of you? Your workload, Condition 2.0, can be thought of as both the quality and quantity of work. Quality refers to the difficulty or complexity of the tasks you have to perform, whereas quantity represents the number of assignments, projects, tasks, and so on that must be completed.

Condition 3.0 assesses the fit between your work and your ability. How well does your job match your skills? You may perceive that the number or complexity of your assignments is (a) beyond, (b) equal to, or (c) below your present capabilities.

Condition 4.0 represents the state of performance, which results from the match or mismatch between your capabilities and your

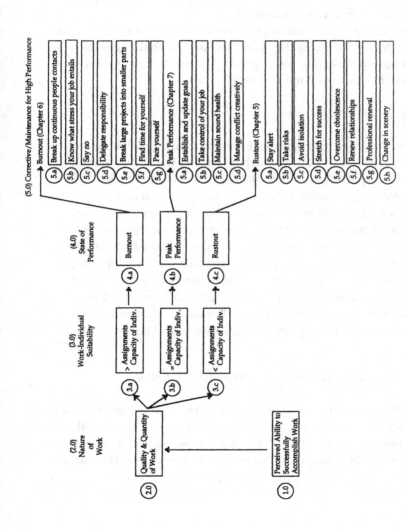

Figure 4.4. Stress and Effective Performance Flow Chart

SOURCE: Adapted from "Stress for Success: How to Optimize Your Performance" by W. H. Gmelch, 1983. *Theory Into Practice, 1,* 7-15.

workload. If you feel your job is over your head, beyond your present abilities, you may suffer from *burnout,* being overemployed in your present job (4.a). If your job does not present you with enough challenge (tasks being relatively simple, routine, and unstimulating), then you may suffer from *rustout* or the underemployment of your skills (4.c). Optimal performance results from the complexity and challenges of your job equaling your capacity. Under this condition, you suffer from neither rustout nor burnout but are optimally stimulated for peak performance (4.b).

Depending on your state of performance, Condition 5.0 suggests some strategies for realigning yourself so your challenges equal or approximate your capabilities, giving you optimum effectiveness. These will be discussed in Chapters 5, 6, and 7.

The Case of Drake Norman

> Drake Norman saw the need to restructure the instructional strategies utilized by his teachers during the early years of his principalship. He fully understood, experienced, and believed in the positive effects of techniques such as cooperative learning within the elementary classroom. Drake set out on an ambitious endeavor to demonstrate the effectiveness of the program. The element of stress inherent in realigning existing practices, developing collaborative working relationships with teachers and staff, and the excitement of potential success coupled with possible failures resulted in an aura of eustress for Drake's work. It was clear that sitting "on the edge" was fueling Drake's enthusiasm and performance.

The Stress and Performance Curve

Note the basic orientation of the stress and performance curve in Figure 4.5: Stress ranges from low to high along the horizontal axis; performance ranges from low to high on the vertical axis; and the curve is more bell-shaped than an inverted U-shape. The curve is divided into three zones of stimulation: under, optimum, and over. Finally, notice the horizontal "life line" slightly above the base of

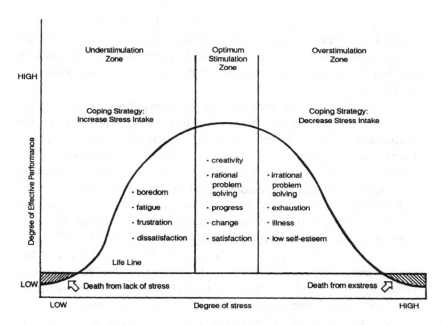

Figure 4.5. Stress and Performance Curve

the graph. These new features suggest several properties of your performance curve to be explored. Let's review these before checking your position on the curve.

1. The Life Line. This life line connotes low to no performance due to too little or too much stress. These are extreme points. On the left side, recall some principals, who, with 15 years of experience in the office, have only one year of experience 15 times over. They may be physically alive, but are professionally dead. At the other extreme you may recognize principals who have gone too long and too hard, and now have gone beyond the burnout stage to a point where they are neither physically nor professionally "alive."

2. Stimulation Zones. The first zone, that of understimulation, can be typified as the trauma of routine and uneventfulness. Principals resting here are underchallenged and suffer from boredom, fatigue, frustration, and dissatisfaction. Principals and teachers resting here too long literally "rust out" from sitting in the same office or class-room without periods of variety, change, or stimulation to keep their motivation high. Either their skills or knowledge become obsolete, leaving them with little or nothing to do that requires excitement or challenge.

At the other extreme rest principals who have been going too hard for too long and now find themselves burned out. Here we find the ambitious, aggressive, and impatient principals who have not yet learned their limitations. They become irrational problem solvers, exhausted from working long hours, dissatisfied from working without results, and despondent from loss of self-esteem.

School systems concern themselves most with the extremes of rustout and burnout. However, be careful not to overreact. Stress, in itself and in the proper amounts, is not bad. Stress is much like your body's temperature; you must have it to stay alive. You call the doctor and apply treatment only when temperatures run above or below normal. The prescription is logical: increase the stress intake (take on more heat) when understimulated, and decrease stress intake (get out when it's too hot) when overstimulated. The goal in the middle zone is to keep performance at peak levels by creating the right amount of stress to function under optimum stimulation. Here is where principals engage in rational problem solving, creativity, productive change, progress, and real job satisfaction.

3. *Individualized Curves.* Principals may differ considerably in their preferred levels of stimulation and stress. Predicting what level of stimulation suits you best is a matter of evaluating the amount of stress you are used to and the level of stress you are subjected to at one time. For example, if you are accustomed to taking many risks and confronting others, you may not become particularly excited over a dispute with an upset student or a disenchanted teacher. However, another principal who deals less with conflict might find the teacher confrontation quite threatening. While your reaction to the situation may be mild, the other principal's may be extreme.

4. *Burnout Versus Rustout.* The equal size and proportion of the understimulation and overstimulation zones does not imply that equal numbers of principals can be found in each zone, or that similar

dangers exist between being rusted-out and being burned-out. While stress underload afflicts significant numbers of educators, the problem of too much stress plagues an even greater number of principals. However, being burned-out is not worse than being rusted-out. The opposite holds true. Most principals feel they would rather wear out than rust out. It is far more serious to err in the direction of too little pressure than too much. "The Tale of Two Frogs" tells the story:

Two frogs fell into a deep bowl . . .
One was an optimistic soul,
But the other took the gloomy view . . .
"We shall drown," he cried, "without more ado!"
So with a last despairing cry,
He flung up his legs, and said, "Good-bye!"
The other frog with a merry grin . . .
"I can't get out, but I won't give in.
I'll just swim around till my strength is spent,
Then I'll die more content."
Bravely he swam till it would seem,
His struggles began to churn the cream.
On top of the butter at last he stopped,
And out of the bowl he gaily hopped.
WHAT OF THE MORAL? ('tis easily found)
IF YOU CAN'T HOP OUT, KEEP SWIMMING AROUND!
(*Author unknown*)

5. *The Dynamic Curve.* Don't view this curve as simplistic or static. Educators can't be classified as either continually burned-out or continually rusted-out. Everyone fluctuates up and down between zones, depending on the type of activity (burned-out on paperwork but peaked out on kids), and the period of time (daily, weekly, monthly, or yearly cycles). For example, some principals may just be getting warmed up by 8:00 a.m., starting the ascent up the stress curve to their peak period of the day. By 4:00 p.m., some may be sliding down the stress curve into a state of organizational burnout. But being burned-out at the end of the day does not necessarily mean you have to enter your front door at home in the same condition. The optimum stimulation zone can and should vary from one part

of your life to the next. Many temporarily burned-out or rusted-out principals find revitalization in their hobbies and special interests.

The trick is to know where you are on the curve, when you are at optimum performance, and how to stay at peak performance over long periods of time. The next sections will respond to each of these areas.

The Rustout–Burnout Syndrome

Recall the conclusion of the Little League study: Optimum performance results from the interaction of the task difficulty, the player's ability, and the state of arousal. The level of stress or arousal depends on one's perception of his/her ability to fulfill the task or assignment. In order to assess the amount of difficulty or challenge your job entails, you must check your perception of the workload against your ability to accomplish it. Once you assess the suitability of your job to your abilities, you can then take positive action to optimize your performance.

The following questionnaire (titled the RO-BO Scale, for Rustout/Burnout) is designed to provide you with information to compare your present level of work with your ideal level of work. Read the 10 pairs of statements and indicate in statement "a" of each pair what you are presently expected to do on your job. Indicate in statement "b" what you feel you are ideally capable of doing. Be realistic about what you are capable of doing. As a rule, number 3 (average) is intended to represent the abilities of an average principal.

Scoring Your RO-BO Scale

The odd-numbered pairs of statements (1, 3, 5, 7, and 9) of the RO-BO Scale represent the *quantitative* (number of assignments) dimension of your present workload, while the even-numbered pairs of statements (2, 4, 6, 8, and 10) represent the *qualitative* (difficulty of assignments) dimension of your workload.

Exercise 4.1

RO-BO Scale

Based on the Response Scale below, assign each "a" and "b" statement a response score. Then subtract the number in statement "a" from the number in statement "b" and write the difference in the Sum column. Be sure to use a plus or minus sign to indicate whether the first statement received a higher or lower score than the second.

Response Scale

Little or None	Some	Average	A Lot	A Great Deal	Sum
1	2	3	4	5	
1	2	3	4	5	

Statement   Sum

1. a. The number of deadlines I have to meet
   b. The number of deadlines I am capable of meeting   ___

2. a. The degree to which my skills are used
   b. The degree to which my skills could be used   ___

3. a. The number of tasks I have to do
   b. The number of tasks I am capable of doing   ___

4. a. The level of difficulty of my work
   b. The level of difficulty I am capable of doing   ___

5. a. The amount of work I have to do in an ordinary day
   b. The amount of work I am capable of doing in an
      ordinary day   ___

6. a. The quality of work I have to do
   b. The quality of work I am capable of doing   ___

7. a. The number of people I have to work with to get
      my job done
   b. The number of people I would like to work with
      to get my job done   ___

8. a. The difficulty of decisions that is expected of me
   b. The difficulty of decisions that I am capable of making ___

9. a. The multitude of "hats" that I am expected to wear in
      my job
   b. The multitude of "hats" that I am capable of wearing
      in my job   ___
10. a. The scope and responsibility of my job
    b. The scope and responsibility I am capable of handling   ___

To calculate your total score for each dimension, add the Sum scores of the Quantitative and the Sum scores of the Qualitative questions together, as shown below

(Questions)   (1) (3) (5) (7) (9)
(Sum scores) ___ + ___ + ___ + ___ + ___ = Quantitative Workload

(Questions)   (2) (4) (6) (8) (10)
(Sum Scores) ___ + ___ + ___ + ___ + ___ = Qualitative Workload

The significance of the total score in each of the two dimensions varies from individual to individual. It is possible to score from −20 to +20 on each dimension.

The Principal Stress and Performance Curve provides you with a guideline to gain a perspective on each total score. As an indication of where you are on the curve, mark your dimension scores on the continuums at the base of the Rustout-Burnout Scale in Figure 4.6. Then draw a vertical line up to the corresponding point on the curve. This gives you a general point of reference as to which zone of performance you may currently be working within. Are you burning out, rusting out, or at peak performance?

Interpreting Your Results

To help you interpret your scores, let's review a hypothetical middle school with 800 students, 35 teachers, 5 clerical staff/secretaries, and an assistant principal. One might find that the principal's qualitative job is satisfying (2 on the scale and within the optimum performance zone). Her skills are apparently being challenged in her present position. However, the number of reports and forms she

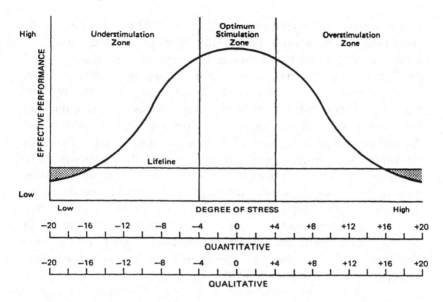

Figure 4.6. Rustout-Burnout Scale

is responsible for appears to be overwhelming (+13 score). Conversely, the teachers have found the right mix in the number of classes they are carrying (–1 score), but they are still in need of more challenging work (–10 score). The same pattern exists with the secretary and assistant principal; they have plenty to do in terms of the number of responsibilities but do not feel challenged.

What can be done to increase productivity in this school? Some educators need to reduce stress in certain areas and increase it in others. The first clue would be what they are presently doing, not necessarily how their assignments read. Recognizing the problems with case study oversimplification, one solution would be to have the principal delegate his or her responsibility to coordinate facility usage to the assistant principal, to reduce the quantitative load and increase the assistant principal's challenge with a new set of exciting responsibilities.

The secretary evidently has plenty to do in terms of the number of tasks she has to perform, but she is currently feeling under-challenged with the low level of complexity or difficulty of the tasks.

Some are probably routine and simplistic. The principal, under these circumstances, should try to substitute tasks with more responsibility and give her the authority to carry out these tasks to completion, such as the maintenance and budgeting of office supplies and equipment. The clerical assistants all seem to be suffering from the same discontent: boredom from repetitious assignments. Currently their work is divided by function: attendance and the like. To add variety to their jobs and gain an understanding of the entire operation, they might rotate jobs or redesign their assignment by academic department, rather than function, so that one clerical assistant, as an example, would oversee all the clerical needs of the special education department. This would include budget control, staffing needs, instructional supplies, coordination, and so on. By giving support staff the opportunity to build variety and interest into their work, the school principal would find an increase in both staff performance and satisfaction.

The scenario above involved job-change solutions to low-performance problems. Principals may have a variety of these techniques available to them in terms of promotion, reassignment, job redefinition, relocation, and, of course, dismissal. Another range of alternatives exists in terms of training and development in the areas of skills training, educational programming, career counseling, and even personal counseling. How you and your school select and apply these alternatives depends on the circumstances and personnel involved. However, the application of a proper solution to a performance problem should not be left to happenstance nor be approached in a piecemeal fashion. One study of a dozen major corporations discovered that none had a systematic program of helping managers get back on the performance track through involvement, commitment, and personal growth. In all instances their solutions ranged from nominal promotions and early retirement to dismissal.

Rustout

In Search of Change and Challenge

The Case of Norm Washington

Norm Washington is in his 12th year as the principal of Central Plains Elementary School. He began his educational career more than 26 years ago as a second-grade teacher within the same school system. A colleague of Norm's would often reminisce about the "good old" days when Norm and several of his colleagues would gather in the faculty lounge and dream of exciting and creative ways to group and assess elementary students. District personnel can be heard saying Norm was perhaps the "pioneer of cooperative science education" at the elementary level. That was 12 years ago.

Riding on his enthusiasm and successes, Norm applied for and became the inside candidate for the elementary principalship, vying against a pool of four external candidates. The search committee unanimously agreed that

Norm Washington would be the one best suited and qualified for the position.

The early years of principalship at Central Plains Elementary School were complete with building-wide dialogues revolving around multiple age grouping, cooperative learning, and age-appropriate curriculum. To Norm's credit, even the more tenured staff remained open to the new direction and focus of the school. Staff development and in-service were made available; Norm was constantly visiting classes to help the teachers toward instructional improvement; and when teachers retired, they were deliberately replaced with teachers enthusiastic and impassioned with the philosophy of whole-child learning. It would not be uncommon to overhear teachers talking about Norm's early years as the most exciting and dramatic in the school's history.

The years passed by, and while Norm continued to articulate his platform of cooperative learning, the audience for his message eroded. Student demographics dramatically altered the population attending Central Plains. The redefinition of district lines, combined with the state's open enrollment policy, created a very different school from the one in the early 1980s. The faculty and staff at Central Plains have changed, through attrition and transfers, and the heyday of rapid instructional innovation is now only a memory. The agenda currently facing the school includes issues of child abuse, substance usage, social agency interventions, child care opportunities, and parenting education.

Central Plains teachers have shunned discussions of instructional innovations and are demanding greater support services from site and district administration. Norm Washington's role has drastically shifted from being a catalyst for professional dialogue to one of dealing with reams of paperwork, coordinating the efforts of community agencies and the school, and acting as the buffer when angry parents demand greater student services. Critics of Norm Washington's performance have said, for example, that Norm has lost his competitive edge amidst the current demands for his school, and that he can no longer provide the leadership to move his school and faculty toward resolving the issues facing the school. Norm laments the changes within his position and role, saying, "I come to work now and sit in my office and shuffle papers all day. Between signing and writing state and district reports, wrestling with the budget, and meeting with social agencies, where do I find the time to talk about learning? I don't even know if that's something I should be doing now. I really don't blame anybody, but in reality I don't know why I'm still here. Maybe it's time to go."

The Treatment of Low Performance

Applying a treatment to low-performing Norm Washington in the above case is difficult. Solutions are not obvious and have not been well articulated. Organizations have not done enough to diagnose and prescribe techniques to aid low or plagued performers, that is, besides the traditional method of produce or be fired, retired, or relocated. This chapter will provide you with treatments, techniques, and strategies for maximizing performance. First, treatments for the qualitative and quantitative stages of rustout will be provided. They include (a) motivation by objectives for qualitative rustout, and (b) job enrichment for quantitative rustout. Following these treatment procedures, several techniques will be shared for rustout prevention, to help you maintain your high performance curve.

Motivation by Objectives: The Cure for the Underemployed

Management by Objectives (MBO) has been around since the late 1940s, most recently popularized in the 1960s. Most principals have heard of MBO and few argue against this system, which promotes more objective evaluation, tighter control, more accurate planning, and improved communication. Few, however, realize the power of *motivation* that lies behind a successfully implemented MBO plan. Instead of the old Management by Objectives, a properly implemented Motivation by Objectives plan could turn rusted-out Norm Washington into a blossoming star performer.

Exercise 5.1

Motivation by Objectives

Goal: To increase job effectiveness and performance.

1. Key Responsibilities	2. Indicators	3. Target Dates	4. Results
1.	1.		
2.	2.		
3.	3.		
4.	4.		

At the risk of oversimplification, the following process characterizes the key ingredients of a successful Motivation by Objectives plan—one that will keep you and your employees challenged, motivated, and resistant to settling in one place too long and rusting out.

Step 1: Have you and your staff list your specific areas of responsibilities. Some typical areas are:

- support ongoing evaluation of teachers
- staff development
- community relations
- maintenance of school vision
- budget control
- staff evaluation
- instructional leadership

Step 2: Gain agreement with your superintendent on which responsibilities you wish to target for the next 6 months to a year. Then list these key responsibilities in Column 1 of the Motivation by Objectives worksheet in Exercise 5.1.

Step 3: Develop indicators of successful completion of the objectives. Just like golf, you and your supervisor need to know what is par for the course. It should also be published on a scorecard. So, list the benchmarks of successful completion in Column 2. Be sure to set both quantity and quality indicators, since it is easy to cut quality at the expense of quantity and vice versa.

Step 4: Establish a periodic feedback system to check your progress on meeting your objectives. Indicate these dates and the results of your efforts in Columns 3 and 4. Without specific deadlines you may be left with "good intentions," which may have produced the rust-out condition in the first place.

Step 5: Hold follow-up review sessions with your supervisor. Set them up at 30-day intervals, or possibly longer, to allow you time to experiment and see some results of your efforts.

You will be amazed with the results (1) if you provide a positive climate for growth, (2) if these simple but essential steps are followed, and (3) if enough time and patience are provided to allow you or your employees to pull yourselves out of the doldrums and place yourselves on top of the performance curve. Talents are like muscles; they grow with use.

Job Enrichment: The Cure for Not Enough to Do

While excessive stimulation creates burnout, the lack of it contributes to boredom. If you scored in the − 4 to −20 range on the quantitative continuum of the RO-BO Scale in Chapter 4, you may be suffering from too little meaningful work.

The most significant and most overlooked responsibility principals have is their personal growth and job enrichment. This critical source of stimulation and motivation typically is left to the inertia of the past, the happenstance of the present, or the whim of the future.

Job enrichment should delve into the past, assess the present, and plan for the future. The following questions serve as a guide for your employees to take assessment of their strengths so together you can set targets for the future. Have them reflect and write their answers to these questions:

1. What jobs in education or elsewhere have I held?
2. Which jobs did I do best? Why?

Exercise 5.2

Skill Interest Inventory

	I Can	I Am	I Would Like to	Our Plan Is
1.				
2.				
3.				
4.				
5.				
6.				
7.				
8.				
9.				
10.				

3. Which jobs did I do least well? Why?

4. Which jobs did I enjoy the most? Why?

5. Which jobs did I enjoy least? Why?

Now have them list the particular skills they have developed over their careers on the form in Exercise 5.2. This is their list of "I can": I can work with people; I can write; I can talk in front of groups; I can program computers; I can read financial statements; I can analyze problems; and so on.

Next to each skill or "I can" item, have your employees indicate their "I am": What they are presently doing in their jobs in each of the skill areas. For example, "I am currently keeping the books on small capital outlays." Now have them compare the two lists to look for gaps or deficiencies between what they are capable of doing and what they are currently doing.

Here is where you can capitalize and build enrichment into their jobs. For each skill area or "I can" category that is not fulfilled sufficiently (either nothing or little done) by an "I am" activity, indicate in the third column "I would like to" tasks.

Finally, sit down with an employee and review the Skill Interest Inventory. Agree on additional assignments he or she can add to the job. Write the plan down in the fourth column so both of you understand what is to be done.

For example, Linda, the school secretary, keeps very busy during the day until 3:00 p.m., when the workload slackens to almost nothing. She is happy and productive most of the time, but when late afternoon rolls around, she begins to fall into a valley of despair from nothing to do. By having Linda complete the Skill Interest Inventory, the principal found out that Linda "can" perform many tasks and responsibilities, such as desktop publishing, computer database maintenance, and so on. She currently is not asked to use her skills in this area, but she indicates she "would like to" use her desktop publishing skills. Since Linda completes her tasks early in the day, she and the principal agreed that she should take responsibility for creating a biweekly newsletter for the school.

Sound far-fetched? I doubt it. Once I lost an excellent secretary to the rustout syndrome. She didn't have enough to do and I didn't know it. The Skill Interest Inventory would have been a helpful starting point for discussion and enrichment of her job. I think we all agree that there is nothing more devastating and demoralizing than helplessly rusting out of your job.

For further work in the area of job enrichment, consult Richard Bolles' *What Color Is Your Parachute?* (1979) and *The Three Boxes of Life* (1978). These are particularly helpful resources.

Coping With Rustout

1. Stay Alert. Participate in special interest activities (hobbies and pastimes not related to your job) to promote self-confidence and competence in areas outside your profession. Find activities that provide you with meaning, reward, and satisfaction. As a starting point, the Coping Response Inventory in Chapter 7 lists more than 100 activities principals claim have helped them overcome the stress of work.

2. Take Risks. Be bold and take enough risks so that your skills are challenged, but not so many that you are overwhelmed. Remember, a turtle makes progress only when it sticks its neck out. We are all anxious to achieve security, growth, and fulfillment. Growth and productivity result from taking risks. Stagnation emanates from not seeking challenges. Don't fear failure. As Will Rogers astutely put it: "Even if you are on the right track, you'll get run over if you just sit there."

3. Avoid Isolation. Under duress many begin to withdraw from social interaction with their staff members, friends, and family. Isolation can draw you further into depression, so keep the communication lines open with your colleagues and friends.

4. Stretch for Success. Probably the most important relationship is the one between stress and success. People are not highly motivated if they view goals as either almost impossible or a cinch. Motivation is highest when there is a 50% probability of success—it keeps you on your toes, stretching for success. Any coach knows a team performs best when there are even odds of winning, or that "on any given day any given team can beat another." We always need hope, for without hope there is no desire.

5. Overcome Obsolescence. In times of rapid change and technological advances, a principal's skills acquired in pre-service college courses quickly become obsolete if not updated through on-the-job-training opportunities. Probably one of the greatest fears today is that of becoming obsolete or dated in our professions. Avail yourself of the numerous training opportunities to make sure you become periodically updated on the newest thinking in the field. Keep yourself on the cutting edge of knowledge. As one management expert says, "If the job is as comfortable as an old shoe, you're not allowing for growth."

6. Renew Relationships. Often the isolation of the principalship magnifies the difficulties of the position. Several principals have found that by joining area collegial groups of similar colleagues, the isolation can be broken and a sense of peer support can be nurtured. Having other principals share success as well as failures can tremendously soothe the often rough rides principals embark on. The value of collegial groups lies in the identification of peers who often share common issues, situations, and challenges.

In addition, the collegial group is an exciting avenue to begin developing relationships outside of the school building, often lending a refreshing and exciting perspective to situations and problem-solving exercises.

7. Professional Renewal. Districts have adopted staff renewal programs in an effort to maintain their employees on the cutting edge. Roseville school district in Minnesota has identified teachers who are close to retiring and has offered them the opportunity to become mentors for newly hired staff. Release time is provided by the district to the mentors for meetings, research, observations, and curriculum writing. Another exciting program being developed brings practitioners in to the University of St. Thomas, Minnesota, to serve as adjunct instructors for a semester or more. The district would work collaboratively with the university to provide coverage and release time.

The value of staff renewal programs is not in the tasks or roles teachers assume, but rather in the divergent set of parameters and boundaries inherent within their changing arena of responsibilities. Common to each of the programs described is the challenge of having teachers work with colleagues and the venue to tap into their collective base of expertise and experiences.

8. Change in Scenery. The simple task of changing scenery, both geographically and in professional roles, has been beneficial to many principals. These principals have either collectively or individually engaged in one of the following:

1. Travel to do research on different educational systems.
2. Travel to do graduate study at a university.
3. Travel to pursue a hobby or passion, such as an eco-tour.
4. Travel to a teacher exchange in an overseas school.

You will notice that prevention strategies for rustout will be different from the ones suggested in the next chapter on burnout prevention. Rustout prevention plans suggest techniques to increase the intake of stress by cultivating outside interests, seeking companionship, avoiding isolation from your staff, seeking support, taking risks, and changing the scenery. As you can see, the philosophy of rustout prevention rests on the assumption of increasing the amount of stress in the principalship; in other words, trying to move you from the rustout end zone into the middle for high performance.

Burnout

Going Beyond Your Peak

A Day in the Life of Gayle Martinez

Gayle Martinez was the first non-Anglo principal hired by the Hoskin Unified School District. Her extensive background in Chicano studies and English as a Second Language programs made her a "custom ordered" candidate for the position at Hoskin High School. The demographics of the school included a 42% Hispanic population, followed by a 22% Asian student body. Eight years ago, Gayle saw the opportunity to work in this diversity-rich environment as fulfillment of a lifelong dream. Since that time, her dream has become an albatross.

Driven by her personal desire to affect attitudinal and emotional change among the students and faculty, Gayle typically worked 60-hour weeks to develop programs, practices, and policies consistent with an inclusive approach to education. She met weekly with a group of students to discuss cultural issues, a group of parents to discuss parenting skills and school support, and finally, a group of faculty to work through modifying current delivery systems. On top of these meetings, Gayle would be available for all the athletic and fine arts activities, to show physical support to her students. It would not be uncommon to see Gayle's car in the parking lot at 6:30 a.m. and again at 6:30 p.m.

Gayle's approach to leadership was by example. She would aggressively volunteer for almost every committee, task force, and social gathering. In addition, she would personally see students for disciplinary issues, rather than fully utilize her administrative staff. She felt dedicated and fully responsible for turning the school around. Predicated on this personalization of task, Gayle has also offered her time to collaboratively work with teachers on modifying their teaching strategies, an approach that often pulls her into classes on a daily basis. As a result of her open-door policy, the school day is no longer under the control of Gayle. Rather, teachers, students, staff, and parents take advantage of filling Gayle's day with appointments, both scheduled and informal. The paperwork of operating a high school remains on her desk, often taking her into the evening to complete.

Compounding the difficulties of Gayle's position is the pressure from the faculty to move off her agenda, juxtaposed with the pressure from central office to begin moving Hoskin High School toward a model of site-based management. Six years of operating on overdrive, coupled with little visible change, have severely crippled Gayle's perspective. While she continues to drive herself, faculty at Hoskin High School have abdicated the day-to-day responsibility for student self-esteem and have labeled this task "Gayle's thing." Gayle has personally taken on every conceivable role of counselor, disciplinarian, surrogate parent, friend, and teacher to her students in an effort to reach those few falling through the cracks. The difficult part of this is her deep-seated passion for her work, combined with the emptiness of doing it alone.

Over the past year, Gayle has begun to see the futility of her labor. Increasing her energies to effect teacher change has had the effect of pushing the teachers away. Offering her time and help to faculty and staff has resulted in animosity and resentment. Driving home the nurturing aspect of school has only swayed the faculty and the central office to move in other directions. Paying attention to "real" student needs has shackled Gayle to her desk until the late evening hours. Gayle's enormous task is similar to stopping a tidal wave with your hands. After the crest of water, Gayle needs to look awfully hard to find dry land. She is very close to giving up.

Clearly Gayle Martinez has been on fire—and is now close to burnout. Schools have not recognized either the symptoms or the consequences of burnout on the performance of principals. The subsequent sections of this chapter will provide you with treatments, techniques, and strategies for decreasing burnout and maximizing performance. First, treatments for qualitative and quantitative stages of burnout suggest (a) diagnosing and dealing with performance problems and (b) identifying high-payoff tasks and setting priorities. Following these treatments, several techniques will be provided to prevent burnout in the future.

Stages and Symptoms of Burnout

The consequences of excessive stress lead to long-range effects on principals' health and performance. In addition to the physiological ailments of headaches, ulcers, illnesses, or disabilities, some researchers have separated the psychological consequences of stress into three stages of burnout: emotional exhaustion, depersonalization, and personal accomplishment (Maslach & Jackson, 1981).

Emotional Exhaustion

Emotional exhaustion occurs when principals' emotional resources are depleted and they feel they are no longer able to give of themselves at a psychological level. At this stage principals feel fatigued, frustrated with their job, and emotionally drained from working at school. As was the case with Gayle Martinez, this exhaustion originates in excessive psychological and emotional demands made on principals to interact with others. The term *exhaustion* connotes a demanding job with continuous arousal—typical of what Gayle Martinez has experienced.

Depersonalization

The second symptom of burnout, depersonalization occurs when principals feel negative and cynical attitudes about students, staff, and faculty. A depersonalized principal treats students like objects and may label them or use "distancing" adjectives or pronouns instead of using their names. Principals at the depersonalization stage may not really care what happens to faculty. They may exhibit signs of detachment and feel callous and cynical toward their colleagues.

Personal Accomplishment

Principals with low personal accomplishment evaluate them-selves negatively and become dissatisfied with their accomplish-ments in the building. Principals who repeatedly fail to produce desired results, such as Gayle's attempt to move toward site-based management, develop symptoms of stress and depression. Even-tually, they believe their actions no longer make a difference and give up trying.

In a recent study of administrative burnout and levels of school administration, elementary, middle school, and high school prin-cipals experienced significantly higher levels of emotional exhaus-tion and had lower levels of personal accomplishment than super-intendents (Torelli & Gmelch, 1993). While that is the bad news, the good new is that principals in this study showed lower levels of burnout than other professionals in the human services area. Over-all, principals at all levels are hardy leaders.

The Hardy Principal

Why do some principals exhibit this resilience to burnout? A few clues have emerged regarding psychological qualities that may help account for this resilience to burnout. Suzanne Kobasa began by studying the health of 670 middle- to upper-level managers (Kobasa,

Hilker, & Maddi, 1979). She found managers with high stress but low illness to be more actively involved in their work and social lives. They believed they were more in control of the events in their lives, had a greater sense of commitment to life beyond their profession, and viewed changes in their lives as challenges. Let's explore the three Cs that principals may use to guard against burnout.

Control

Hardy principals believe they can affect their school and environment. Rather than thinking that stress will kill them, they take charge and choose among various courses of action to defuse threatening stressful events.

Challenge

The hardy principals see change as an opportunity for challenge. Change can be the spice of life, and hardy principals believe education will always present problems. Once a problem is identified, they see it as an opportunity to make schools more effective.

Commitment

While accepting challenge, hardy principals have the ability to become committed to school and personal life. They become active and interested in life's opportunities. They are more likely to identify the important aspects of life and commit themselves to these goals.

In summary, hardy principals are those who are involved and committed, who believe they control their own lives, and who see change as an opportunity rather than a threat. Burned-out principals who fall ill, on the other hand, feel overwhelmed and powerless to cope, see the world as worthless, have an aversion to change, and perceive security as the status quo.

The Stress Survivor Principal

But why is it that under crisis some principals survive and others collapse? Some of the answer lies in the principal's personality. A stress survivor personality can sustain high levels of pressure and still perform well (Siebert, 1980). When faced with crisis, the stress survivor counterattacks with a sequence of responses that use stress to produce positive results, not burnout.

1. Find Some Humor. When a crisis hits, the stress survivor doesn't panic, but finds some humor in the situation, which calms the emotions rather than adding to emotional exhaustion. This does not mean to laugh the problem off, but to have a good joke, lighten up, and put the problem in perspective.

2. Have a Private Saying. A private saying may come from one's religious or philosophical beliefs. They tend to keep us on course, or throw out an anchor in the wind. Examples of catchy sayings some principals use to steer themselves back on course are:

- The road to success is always under construction.
- When life hands you a lemon, make lemonade.
- When under attack, circle the wagons.
- There is no gain without pain.
- Life by the mile is a trial, by the yard is hard, by the inch it's a cinch.

3. Relax and Put the Crisis in Perspective. This does not mean to go home, go to sleep, and ignore the problem, but sit back and spend a few minutes in contemplation before charging ahead with an action you may later regret.

Use these first three steps to help clear your mind before taking any action. Then proceed to the next four steps.

4. Ask Questions. The more you know about the problem, the easier it may be to find a solution. Go out and probe sources of information about the crisis at hand. This technique acts as a burnout resister.

5. See the Crisis as a Challenge. This action represents a change of mind or attitude about the problem. Look at the crisis not as a problem to be avoided, but as a potential opportunity to work to your advantage—for "every pearl is the result of an oyster's victory over an irritation." So make some pearls out of some problems.

6. *Find Creative Solutions.* Once we see a solution, we tend to lock in on it and find it difficult to consider other alternatives. Psychologists call these *skitomas,* or blind spots. The stress survivor principal goes beyond the logical solutions and looks for unusual or creative ones. This involves not only searching the left side of the brain, what is now called the logical side, but also switching to the creative right side for opportunities that, at first glance, might be overlooked.

7. *Maintain Your Flexibility.* The first six steps in stress survival represent a sequence of activities found to be helpful in combating what normally could lead to burnout. However, there exists a seventh part to the stress survival scheme for principals. Take a minute and check off the traits below that typically represent you. Read down the first column and then the second. Remember, there are no right or wrong answers, so just check the ones that typically characterize yourself.

_____ tender	_____ tough
_____ shy	_____ outgoing
_____ mature	_____ childlike
_____ emotional	_____ rational
_____ serious	_____ humorous
_____ feminine	_____ masculine
_____ relaxed	_____ easy-going
_____ creative	_____ practical
_____ tactful	_____ outspoken
_____ leader	_____ follower
_____ individualistic	_____ conforming
_____ self-confident	_____ self-critical
_____ collaborative	_____ competitive

Every surviving creature can move in either of two directions—fight or flight. In the same sense, principals must have flexibility to change their leadership style to meet the situation. While schools profess the need to administer democratically, studies have shown that under crisis conditions, the principal must autocratically take charge and lead.

Review the traits you have checked. The traits in the first column are opposite those in the second. The reason you checked the traits in each column separately is to avoid thinking of yourself as either sensitive or tough, strong or gentle, leader or follower. We tend to think in terms of polar opposites, without room for positions in the middle. Now, look for patterns between the two columns of traits. Did you have pairs of opposite traits checked off in both columns? How balanced or flexible are your traits?

Like animals, we can survive if we have a choice of two directions when confronted. If the only tool you have is a hammer, you will treat all your staff as though they are nails. Some situations call for grace and sensitivity. Your personality can either resist or intensify your chances for burnout.

The Performance Audit:
The Cure for the Overemployed

No matter how well you relate to the stress survivor personality, at times we all feel a bit over our heads. It is natural and, in a sense, all right, since we need to stretch for goals and feel challenged, for neglected muscles atrophy and weaken. In this chapter we are concerned about principals who have reached this level of burnout and have experienced emotional exhaustion, depersonalization, a poor sense of personal accomplishment, or physiological symptoms of excessive stress.

If you found that your score on the qualitative workload part of the RO-BO Scale in Chapter 4 placed you in the overstimulated zone, maybe it is time to assess the fit between your skills and your job requirements. Robert F. Mager and Peter Pipe (1970), in a handy guide called *Analyzing Performance Problems,* take you through a series of questions to find out if you really do have a performance problem (defined as a discrepancy between one's actual performance and one's desired performance).

The first phase of questioning centers around refining your thinking about the performance discrepancy. Ask yourself the questions in Exercise 6.1 about your work performance as principal.

Exercise 6.1

The Performance Audit

---

1. Is there a performance discrepancy? ___ Yes ___ No
   - Why do I think things are not going right? _____
   - What is the difference between what I am producing and what I am supposed to produce? _____
   - Why am I not satisfied with my performance? _____
     _____

2. Is the discrepancy important enough to be worried about? ___ Yes ___ No
   - Why is it important? _____
   - What would happen if I left it alone? _____

3. If the discrepancy were corrected, would it be worth the effort?
   _____

4. Is it a deficiency in my managerial skills? ___Yes ___No
   - Could I perform at the desired level if I really had to? ___ Yes ___ No
   - Are my present skills adequate to obtain the desired results? ___ Yes ___ No
   - Could I do it if my life depended on it? ___ Yes ___ No

After you have asked yourself this battery of questions, you should have an idea of whether your work overload is really a skill deficiency or a problem of motivation. If it is the latter, Mager and Pipe present a series of questions to ascertain why you are not performing at the desired level when you have the skills to do so. Assuming you are not suffering from a problem of motivation, let's proceed with the next questions to examine why the deficiency exists, so you can shape your solution to attack the underlying cause.

5. Have you performed this skill in the past? ___ Yes ___ No
   - Did you at some time know how to perform at the desired level? ___ Yes ___ No

- Have you forgotten how to do what your boss wants you to do? ___ Yes ___ No

If you answered "No" to these questions, you are being asked to perform a skill you have never been trained to do. In this case, seek formal training and assistance. However, if at one time you were able to perform the skill, then move on to the next series of questions.

6. How often have you used this skill? _____
   - Do you get regular feedback on how well you have done? ___ Yes ___ No
   - How do you find out if you are doing well?

   _____

If you find that your skill has been used frequently but has deteriorated, try to increase your performance by asking for periodic feedback on how well you have done. If, on the other hand, you use this skill infrequently, and it is important to maintain, then practice your skill regularly.

You can still determine if there is a simpler solution.

7. Does a solution simpler than formal training or skill practice exist? ___ Yes ___ No
   - Can I rearrange my job requirements by employing some assistance?_____
   - Would on-the-job training be adequate to gain the skills required?_____

Depending on the nature of your answers to all seven categories of questions, you now have a possible set of five solutions: (1) keep a frequently used skill sharp and ready to apply by seeking feedback; (2) practice your skill periodically, if you do not use it often but want to keep it sharp; (3) seek formal training through higher education institutions or professional administrator associations; (4) try to employ on-the-job training practices in your present position; or (5) negotiate a change in your job requirements.

The above series of questions and resolutions to performance problems gives you guidance on how to approach the stress from complex and difficult assignments beyond your present capabilities. You are basically left with three strategies: (1) change your skill level; (2) change your job requirements; or (3) change your job.

When overambition places you in such a position, remember this story:

> There were some carpenters
> They decided to build a house
> They started with the roof
> They had a very hard time
> It kept falling down on them.

Optimum stress and effective performance build up from a foundation of experience and perseverance. The blend of both moves us up to our level of competence.

HIPOS and LOPOS: The Cure for Too Much to Do

If you fell into the overstimulation zone on the RO-BO quantitative workload scale, you are probably suffering from an overload: too many tasks to complete in your normal working day. Interestingly, a study of 60 corporate executives found that 40% of a manager's time is spent in wasteful, unproductive activities involving clerical work, screening information, and checking up on people and projects.

How do we gain some of that time back? The typical time-saving scenario begins by listing all the tasks that need to be completed, setting priorities among the tasks, and scheduling tasks into your calendar in the most efficient order possible. The trouble with this common practice is that we really haven't eliminated any tasks, just reordered them "in the most efficient order." International management expert Peter Drucker gives us a clue as to where to start: Effective executives start with their time, not their tasks (Drucker, 1967).

Think of your time as totally inelastic (we all have 24 hours in a day), totally irreplaceable (we can't turn the clocks back to gain time we've already wasted), and totally committed (everything we do requires time). Sure, you want to be efficient with your time to get more tasks done. Prioritizing and scheduling help, but the critical element is missing: How effective are you with your use of time? That is, not just getting things done, but getting the right things done. We all look efficient shuffling papers, making lists and checking them twice. Instead of reordering and shuffling tasks when you're suffering from burnout, you need to eliminate some; otherwise, you will still be playing with a "stacked deck."

Here's a simple time-management technique that may save you hours of productive time and put your present workload back in perspective. Instead of making "high-priority" lists, try starting with a "high-payoff" list. As we all know, high priority lists are often set by us alone, at the urgent demands of our employees, from a lengthy job description, or just by default. In contrast, a high-payoff list should consist of the critical few hard-to-delegate items that represent the make-or-break functions of your position. Some items may include staff development and training, visioning, program and curriculum development, feasibility studies, and other activities representing the critical components of your job. These are things you should check with your boss periodically, to see if you are doing the "right" things.

Begin by putting away your "to do" list. Now, with a clear mind, take a pad of paper and write down on the first page three to five make-or-break tasks. These are called your HIPOS—high-payoff tasks. They should be easy to identify. But you are not finished yet. Burnout begins with too many tasks. Most things you do, your ego tells you, are important, otherwise you wouldn't be doing them. Right? Low-priority tasks therefore are seldom identified and often represent your enjoyable tasks: opening mail, writing memos, chatting with colleagues, and so on. Now comes the difficult part. On the second page identify at least three low-payoff tasks you are currently doing, but honestly could relegate to the round file or delegate to someone else. These are your LOPOS—low-priority tasks —which, if not identified, will interfere with getting your HIPOS completed.

Once you have accomplished your new set of payoffs, prioritize them as you would have done with your "to do" list and schedule them in the most efficient order. Now you will not only approach your work in an efficient manner but also with an element of effectiveness.

Burnout Prevention

1. Break up Continuous People Contacts. While rustout prevention suggests avoiding isolation, burnout results from the opposite condition—too many people taking up too much of your time. Some principals suffer from what can be called "encounter stress," from continuously dealing with people all day long. For them the opposite remedy provides relief—schedule blocks of time in your day when you can close the door and plan, write, or read without interruption. Your productivity will increase and your tension will decline.

2. Know What Stress Your Job Entails. Don't be caught off guard when you find out the principalship is loaded with stress. Know in advance what stress your job entails; that the demands are high, the challenges great, and the time insufficient. Those who are not prepared for the conflicts and risks inherent to managing people may suffer the most.

Be realistic about your expectations, or suffer the consequences. Doctors recently studied the recovery rate of surgery patients. They tracked three types of patients: those who thought surgery would be a breeze—they'd be out of the hospital in a week; those who anticipated some pain but knew they would recover within a couple of weeks; and those who feared the operation and thought they might take quite some time recovering. Which group do you think recovered the quickest? The middle group—the patients who were realistic about the operation and found few surprises. They were prepared for surgery. Being principal is not meant to be analogous to surgery, but the precondition of being prepared for what awaits you is critical in responding to both operations.

3. Say No. Many principals confuse assertiveness with aggressiveness. Assertiveness merely means speaking up for your personal rights as an individual in a nonthreatening, nonevaluative manner. You don't have to be hostile to be assertive—just firm, forthright, and at times repetitive. For example, when teachers come in the office with monkeys (problems) on their backs, help them think about how to solve the problem. If you don't and they leave the monkeys with you, your room will soon be full of monkeys.

Your staff may enter with the best intentions, but if you are not careful, you will inherit their problems, which, from a training point of view, does them a disservice, and from your point of view puts you out of service. If you have a hard time saying no, try a few of these phrases:

> "That's fine. What do you think you could do about it?"
> "I'm not sure this would be consistent with our mission and goals."
> "If I did this for you, I'm not sure it would be fair to the rest of the staff."
> "I am overcommitted now, and if I accept your offer, I will not be able to fulfill my previous obligations."
> "No, but thank you for asking me."

Many other techniques, such as "fogging" and the "broken record" are presented in Manuel Smith's *When I Say No I Feel Guilty* (1975). If you feel saying no is one area that would help cut back some of your work overload, start there.

4. Delegate Responsibility. Excessive responsibility manifests burnout. Principals fail to delegate responsibility to their staff because they feel indispensable—only they can get the job done right. Wouldn't a little bit less than perfect satisfy most job requirements? By delegating, you also train your staff to take on more responsibility and authority, so they too can feel fulfilled in their jobs. Give yourself a break and your employees a chance. After all, a problem shared is a problem halved. But, make sure you haven't shared too much, so you don't also burn out your staff.

5. Break Large Projects Into Smaller Parts. The thought of a monumental project hanging over your head is enough to burn anyone out before there is even a chance to tackle it. Most projects can be broken into smaller, more manageable components, so break them down and treat each as a separate task, with its own time line and set of requirements. Once projects are divided, you can delegate some components to your staff for their involvement, too. As the adage goes: By the mile it's a trial, by the yard it's hard, by the inch it's a cinch.

6. Find Time for Yourself. Experienced principals will often advocate the practice of blocking time for yourself within your own office space as a time for reflection, reading, and renewal. While this may sound like a feasible plan, the reality of a principal's day is anything but linear and restricted to the appointment calendar. In addition, many principals suggest that while closed doors may shut out visual and auditory distractions, the door does not frame out the mental processes and lists of things and people needing attention. Metaphorically, it is like placing a sheet between a child and candy.

Rather, prudent principals have deliberately taken time off from work during typically "non-slow" times. Principals have taken personal leaves in the middle of a hectic week, or during an intense time of their academic year, only to return refreshed and ready to tackle the tough times with enthusiasm and vigor. Principals have stated that if they wait for things to finally slow down, the personal leave will be primarily used for recovery rather than renewal.

7. Pace Yourself. Principals who are effective in managing their stress for optimal performance often speak of the ability to pace themselves. Similarly, runners who come out of the blocks and expend all their energy at the start seldom have enough to finish the race with a strong kick. Sports scientists have suggested that one additional second faster at the start of the race can affect the race by as much as three seconds slower at the finish.

Experienced principals will often identify long-term tasks and the ones that will require additional resources of time and energies. Allowing for parameters of time lines and the nature of the tasks, regrouping a series of tasks to balance a set of high-demand tasks with those requiring less rigor can assist in maintaining a steady pulse of pressure that is followed by a period of regeneration. Seldom can a principal either sustain peak performance or ride within a performance rut for extended periods without losing that competitive edge.

Notice that prevention strategies for rustout and burnout sometimes suggest much different techniques for reaching optimum performance. Rustout prevention plans suggest techniques to increase the intake of stress by cultivating outside interests, seeking companionship, avoiding isolation from staff members, enlisting staff support, taking risks, stretching for success, and acquiring new skills. In contrast, strategies for preventing burnout are based on reducing the intake of stimulation, breaking up continuous people contacts, recognizing how much stress your job entails, being assertive, delegating more responsibility to your staff, and reducing large projects to smaller components. As you can see, the philosophy of each prevention program rests on different but similar assumptions: to either increase or reduce the amount of stress in one's present occupation. In other words, try to move from either end zone into the middle for high performance.

7

Maintaining Your Peak Performance

The Paula Thompson Story

Paula Thompson is beginning her 14th year as principal of Emmett Junior High School. Prior to Emmett Junior High, she served as the Assistant Principal at the neighboring high school. During the 6 years Paula was there, she began with daily swim workouts prior to the start of the school day. Fourteen years later, Paula continues this program of physical fitness, adding, "I really don't like to swim, but this is one way that I can get my exercise in without sacrificing any more time in the evening. It's gotten to a point that if I don't swim, my body becomes a bit sluggish. In addition, I find that during my laps in the water, my mind is wandering and really quite free to just become reflective and think—it's a great way to begin the day, peaceful and refreshed."

Arriving at work 40 minutes prior to the start of school, Paula continues her reflective mode by reviewing her daily schedule of tasks, meetings, and appointments. This leisurely period is purposefully enhanced by a cup of coffee and a croissant. Anticipating the arrival of students, Paula moves into the corridors to greet them upon arrival. She is very animated and warm, attempting to greet each child and adult entering the building. Teachers who see this time as an opportunity to discuss concerns or issues with Paula are often greeted with a empathetic ear and an invitation for them to secure an appointment with her secretary. Paula is deliberate in not accepting other people's problems while standing out in the halls.

Returning to her office, Paula tells her secretary that she will be unavailable for the for next hour. Closing her door, Paula begins the task of mapping out the curricular direction of the school. She plots the school's goals and priorities over the next 5 years while enveloped in the sounds of a soft radio. During this scheduled study time, Paula has the freedom to read, research, write, and think. Surfacing at the end of an hour, Paula is handed a batch of phone messages that arrived during her study time. She prioritizes the few that she needs to personally call and scribbles responses on those that her secretary will follow up on.

Leaving her office, Paula begins her hour of class visitations. She methodically records the classes she enters on any given day, which allows her to stretch her presence. Paula says, "I keep track of the classes so that I'm certain I visit each class during the course of the year. I know principals who don't record the visits and they end up visiting some classes all the time."

During the lunch hour, Paula is often seen in the faculty lunchroom, sitting with a variety of people. She will often initiate a conversation with those around her regarding the school's goals and directions. Realizing that this is a lunch break for teachers, Paula keeps these conversations light and humorous. In addition, she often asks what they think about this or that, and then sits back to listen. Paula returns to her office at the completion of lunch. She returns to the task of developing a pilot model of multi-aged grouping for middle-level students. This is one of the three long-term goals set collaboratively by Paula and her immediate supervisor for the current school year. The excitement of this goal is the challenge it presents to Paula for researching the concept, fully understanding its implications, and packaging the program for presentation to the faculty. Understanding her own technological limitations, Paula has delegated to one of the assistant principals the responsibility of pictorially diagramming the concept for presentation. The excitement of a collaboratively developed piece is instrumental in keeping Paula on the cutting edge. Paula says, "I've done a lot of things in education, but one thing that I've come to realize is that more brains working can produce a superior product."

One might ask, how can a principal of a 1,200-student junior high find the time to work on long-term projects, rather than simply existing by going from crisis to crisis? Paula would tell you that she has worked out an agreement with her secretarial staff and assistant principals, with respect to matching talents with areas of responsibilities. Paula has moved many of the paper-related day-to-day tasks to the desks of the assistant principals, while taking on some of the more global, long-range planning assignments. In addition, she has given a more liberal rein to her secretarial staff to make specifically identified decisions without needing her authorization. These include issues of attendance, transcripts, office maintenance, and office operations.

Paula closes by suggesting, "It's clear that one person cannot do it all; it's impossible to even suggest they can. What we've done here at Emmett Junior High is identify the areas of responsibilities to the talent, interests, and abilities—not to the position. This simple move has allowed each of us to remain excited about what we do—instead of simply attempting to survive till retirement."

Behind many of Paula Thompson's achievements lies the factor of stress. A moderate amount of stress helped her reach peak performance. However, when stress mounts, principals sometimes enter the danger zone, where counterproductive attitudes and behaviors surface. Psychologically, one can become confused, disoriented, irritable, irrational, apathetic, and emotionally withdrawn. After all, a principal can put out only so many brush fires before eventually burning out.

The previous two chapters represented strategies for pulling yourself out of either the rustout or the burnout zone and putting yourself on top of things at peak performance. Each nonperformance condition requires different techniques, much as we spray Rustoleum to prevent corrosion or apply oil to reduce friction. The objective of this chapter is to show you how to maintain your peak performance as a principal.

Let's now turn our attention to how you maintain your effectiveness. How can you prevent yourself from slipping off again into either less-than-optimal zone? Listed below are some techniques that can be used for preventative maintenance and resistance, first against rustout and then against burnout.

Stabilizing Optimum Performance

Use the strategies for burnout and rustout prevention to help you either increase or cut back your job stress. Once you've maintained your position on top of the Principal Stress and Performance Curve, you have to work at stabilizing your position.

A holistic approach toward developing a stable profile is much like a four-legged table: One of the legs represents a strong set of goals; the second leg your ability to take control of the job; the third a solid foundation of good health, fitness, and nutrition; and the fourth, creative conflict resolution. Together they build a stable table. If any one of these four legs is weak, broken, or out of position, it affects the utility and effectiveness of the other three and the balance of the entire table. All four legs must be strong and in position to keep you in the optimum performance zone.

1. *Establish and Update Goals.* Research emphasizes the importance goals play in maintaining personal and professional satisfaction. Yet one magazine reported that only 3% of the people in the United States have actually written their goals. Therefore, we need to first establish our goals. Second, we must recognize that goals and objec-

tives are not static end points, but change as we pass through the ages and stages of our careers. Thus our goals should be revised and updated seasonally, at different ages of life and during different stages of our career. The importance of having a set of guidelines as a stress filter cannot be overemphasized.

Trade-offs between professional and personal interests are a process by which you can set goals for yourself and your staff, family, and friends. Don't pass this strategy by since it is one of the most important aids for maintaining a successful stress profile and fulfilled life. The position of goal setting at the end, rather than the beginning, of the book is to provide you with a springboard from which to take charge of your stress and your life. Goals will put your life and job back in perspective; for

> If you hold your nose to the grindstone rough,
> And hold it down there long enough,
> You'll soon forget there are such things
> As brooks that babble and birds that sing!
> These three things will your world compose,
> Just you, and a stone, and your darn old nose!
> If I had life to live over, I'd pick more daisies.
> (*Author unknown*)

2. Take Control of Your Job. As you are discovering, control represents the key concept of this book; it rests at the foundation of every effective principal. Improper amounts of stress infiltrate our lives when we lose control, when we let others "pull our strings."

Earlier, the principle of concentrating on HIPOS and delegating or eliminating LOPOS was introduced as one of the many take-control techniques. Many others can be found under the rubric of effective time management: Schedule your tasks, screen your telephone calls, close your door, set priorities, and take time to plan. The basic strategy for managing stress is to find those stressors over which you have some control, then take charge and manage them. This is the basic principle of the Principal Action Plan outlined in Chapter 3. Thus, stress control becomes one of the major avenues leading to a balanced life and puts you on top of the performance curve.

3. Maintain a Foundation of Sound Health, Fitness, and Nutrition. Achieving a high level of performance begins with controlling and managing your job and your life; but maintaining your physical and psychological acuity takes much more than just mental control. You should aim at maintaining high performance through a multiphasic attack. That is, it is not enough just to be mentally alert; your body and mind work together. Much like weight control, it takes more than exercise to lose a few extra pounds. It takes exercising more, eating less, and eating the right foods. Much in the same manner, maintaining a positive posture toward stress begins with a multiphasic attack, which includes exercise, proper nutrition, relaxation, and taking responsibility for one's health and well-being. In essence, live by the ideal of wellness: not just a state of being free from illness, but a way of life that goes beyond being healthy to self-responsibility and the "glow of well-being." The importance of this concept in stress control cannot be overlooked or minimized.

4. Manage Conflict Creatively. Aggressive administrators often welcome the opportunity to charge right into the face of conflict. Type A behavior will also typically lead directly into confrontation, often leaving a wake of bruised personalities and egos. These self-starters are often task-oriented, which in many cases serves as the impetus for direct dialogue, engaging the parties in conflict.

Rather than immediately churning up the "seek and confront" mode of conflict management, Fisher and Ury (1983) suggest refraining and allowing a moment to reflect on the genuine interest or needs of the other parties, rather than their position on the issue. The ability to take a brief interlude within the process often leads to a more comprehensive and robust vision of the scenario, thus allowing for a more inclusive resolution. In addition, the time taken often is just enough for cooler heads to collaboratively work to create options that will satisfy all parties (Gmelch & Miskin, 1993).

Developing a Holistic Coping Profile

While the general literature on coping is significant in volume and diverse in attention, the exact coping process is elusive. Researchers from the disciplines of medicine, psychiatry, clinical psychology, behavioral science, and education have undertaken studies to understand the phenomenon of stress and the coping responses.

The foremost authority on stress, Hans Selye (1976), pointed out that despite everything that has been written and said about stress and coping, there is no ready-made formula that will suit everyone. Since no one technique will suit everyone, how can principals maintain their peak performance?

Some researchers have attempted to prescribe both effective and ineffective techniques, which has resulted in misleading conclusions and advice. Others approach coping with singular trend techniques, such as relaxation, aerobics, biofeedback, or other such stress interventions. When developing a coping strategy, consider the following propositions as a basis for your response to stress.

1. The individual is the most important variable; no one coping technique is effective for all principals in all schools. Therefore, coping techniques must be sensitive to cultural, social, psychological, and environmental differences in individuals.
2. Individuals can't change the world around them, and principals cannot change all the barriers in their schools, but they can change how they relate to them.
3. Individuals who cope best develop a repertoire of techniques to counteract different stressors in different situations. Their repertoire of techniques, hence, should represent a holistic approach toward coping. Nonetheless, are there identifiable categories of coping, which, if used holistically, can help principals systematically address the stress of administration? In answer to this question we asked 1,800 school administrators: "Recognizing that being a principal is demanding, what ways have you found useful in handling the pressures of your job?" (Gmelch & Swent, 1984) The majority of principals cited more than one response. In all, they identified more than 3,000 coping responses. Content analysis of these responses revealed coping techniques that can be grouped into seven coping categories. Rather than prescribe specific techniques, we suggest you review the following categories to see which ones are part of your repertoire (Gmelch & Swent, 1984).

4. Principals indicated *social support* activities helped them break out of stress traps, such as having lunch with colleagues; talking it out with a trusted friend; developing companionship with friends outside the school; and developing a good working relationship with faculty, staff, and students.

5. Principals reported that the following *physical activities* helped break the stress attack: individual sports such as jogging, swimming, walking, hiking, horseback riding, martial arts, golf, skiing, and sailing, as well as the team sports of tennis, racquetball, and basketball.

6. Within the third category, *intellectual stimulation*, principals cited attending professional conferences; teaching at least once a year; and experiencing cultural events, such as theaters and museums.

7. *Entertainment* encompasses the fourth category and includes watching television; going to a movie or out to dinner; getting out of town; and taking a vacation, mini-vacations, or weekend vacations.

8. The fifth category consists of *personal interest* techniques, such as playing a musical instrument, gardening, gourmet cooking, taking a nature hike, working on arts or crafts, creative writing, taking avocational classes, and other personal hobbies unrelated to work. Some cited just plain "dropping out of sight."

9. Principals identified a proliferation of *self-management* techniques they used to cope with the pressures, including delegating authority; planning strategically; effectively and efficiently using time; dealing with conflict constructively; and having an excellent, dedicated secretary and administrative staff.

10. Finally, principals identified numerous coping techniques, which could be categorized simply as supportive *attitudes*. The majority of all the coping responses fell into this important category.

While not one of the responses taken separately presents the answer to coping, if they are taken collectively, principals can view this as a coping taxonomy from which to seek their own stress reduction.

Since coping with stress is a holistic and polytechnic proposition, it is much like weight loss: If one were to exercise more, but eat more too, the results might not be as beneficial as exercising more while cutting back or stabilizing one's diet. In much the same way, effective coping consists of building a repertoire of techniques equally balanced in the social, physical, intellectual, entertainment, managerial, personal, and attitudinal categories. Your goal is to maintain peak performance by adding some of these techniques to your present repertoire of coping responses. It is not the principal who masters one technique who copes most effectively and creatively, but the one who possesses the flexibility to call upon any number of techniques from various sources—physical activity, managerial skills, social support, and so on.

The Coping Response Inventory in Exercise 7.1 contains a comprehensive list of the techniques principals and other educational administrators have found helpful for coping with job stresses. Consider each technique as a potential coping response you can add to your coping repertoire.

Select the ones you would consider to be most effective, take your calendar out, and write them in your daily, weekly, or monthly schedule. For example, a couple of principals in our study realized that their sedentary administrative practices added not only stress to their lives but weight onto their frames, so they pledged to get involved in racquetball three times a week. Not only do they now report less stress, but they have also trimmed off a few pounds and are benefiting from sharper mental acuity.

The holistic coping effect becomes synergistic, providing physical, emotional, and intellectual benefits. Only you can make the final decision. Each principal has his or her own tastes, time schedules, and preferences. Some principals find certain techniques, like therapy sessions once a week with other principals, more helpful than trying to go it alone. You must discover for yourself the activities most agreeable to you in each of the coping categories.

Self-Awareness

The surest way of maintaining your level of high performance (optimum stimulation) is to recognize when you are under either too little or too much stress. If we are sensitive and listen to our bodies, we can detect when we're not performing at the optimum

speed; for "it's not the miles but the mileage" that affects performance. Cars operate most efficiently not at 5 or 10 miles an hour nor
at 70 or 80, but at moderate speeds where they receive optimum fuel
efficiency.

Just as when cars gasp, knock, or ping, we too have early warning
signs when our bodies are not functioning at top efficiency. We call
them "early warning signs" because they let us know something is
not going well, and if we don't give ourselves the care and repair
needed, we may be headed for a major breakdown. These early
warning signs come in the form of bodily and behavioral cues.
Naturally the strategy for alleviating early warning signs would be
to identify those attributable to rustout as contrasted to those from
burnout. Paradoxically, many of the early warning signs of stress
underload are quite similar to those of stress overload. For example,
fatigue, dissatisfaction, sleeplessness, and absenteeism result from
being either overstimulated or under-stimulated. Use your own
perception, as well as a review of your score on the Rustout/Burnout
Scale, to know which strategy for recovery should be used.

Most of us have become immune or insensitive to these early
warning signs. We need to listen more to our bodies and behaviors
for these signs. Since no amount of discussion can do justice to the
exact meaning of "listening to your body," the following is an
illustration:

> Make your hand into a fist. Squeeze your hand as hard as
> you can and feel the tension. If you hold the fist tight for
> even a few minutes, your hand will ache with the effort.
> Such a tensed, strained fist has few (peaceful) uses.
>
> Next, drop your hand to your side. Keep all your muscles
> as loose as possible. You can't get much productive work
> out of your hand in that position either.
>
> Now raise your hand slowly in front of you and make it
> come alive. Gradually move the fingers and feel the muscles
> respond with good tone and control. Here is a hand that can
> get something done.

The tone that is neither too tight nor too loose will help get things done. The balanced middle zone produces spontaneous responses to principals' challenges.

Conclusion

You should now be in control of your principal stress cycle. The first part of this book helped you recognize and resolve your stress by (1) checking what it is and where it comes from, (2) identifying stress traps unique to school principals, and (3) resolving your stress traps with the Principal Action Plan. Subsequent chapters then explained how stress affects your performance, specifically, how to prevent rustout and burnout and maintain optimum performance. The next step is yours. Remember the wise Chinese adage: "To know, and not to use, is not yet to know." The material in this book is now yours to know and use. May stress be the spice of your life.

Exercise 7.1

Coping Response Inventory

The Coping Response Inventory (CRI) is designed to assess the methods you use in response to stress. It was developed from our study of more than 1,800 school administrators, who were asked to identify ways they personally found useful in handing the tensions and pressures of their jobs (Gmelch, 1988). The CRI represents a final listing of techniques that comprehensively incorporate all of the principals' coping responses. They are categorized in seven major areas: (1) social support, (2) physical activities, (3) intellectual stimulation, (4) entertainment, (5) personal interest, (6) self-management, and (7) coping attitudes.

Assessing Your Coping Responses

Read each of the items in the CRI and indicate how often, if at all, you use the techniques. Write the appropriate response number in the frequency column as follows:

Frequency Scale:
0 = Never
1 = Once a year or less
2 = Four times a year or less
3 = Monthly
4 = Weekly
5 = Daily

For example, Item 1 in the Social Support category is "talk on the phone with a friend." If you find the only time you call on your friends socially is on the weekend, then you would place a score of "4," for weekly, in the frequency column next to Item 1. Count the number of times you have done any of the activities in Exercise 7.1 and indicate the frequency.

1. Social Item   Frequency
    1. Talk on phone with a friend
    2. Share frustrations with spouse
    3. Give undivided attention to family
    4. Have lunch with family or friends
    5. Give presents and gifts
    6. Confront people directly
    7. Play with kids
    8. Write notes of appreciation
    9. Tell jokes and stories
    10. Visit relatives and friends
    11. Console sick or less fortunate people
    12. Participate in community activities
    13. Attend business, civic, social meetings
    14. Have an open and honest conversation
    15. Make a new friend
    16. Play cards, games (checkers, Scrabble)
    17. Others
        Social Subtotal   _____
        Comments:

2. Physical Activity Item   Frequency
    1. Go boating, sailing, canoeing
    2. Shoot baskets, hit golf balls
    3. Play team sports (soccer, basketball)
    4. Relax with meditation, yoga
    5. Stroll through parks, shops
    6. Go fishing, hunting, shooting
    7. Coach sports (high school, Little League)
    8. Get adequate sleep
    9. Play court sports (tennis, squash)
    10. Do heavy manual work
    11. Talk a brisk walk
    12. Box or wrestle
    13. Go bowling
    14. Exercise
    15. Ride bike
    16. Play pool, billiards
    17. Have sex

18. Play water sports   Frequency
19. Play mountain sports
20. Run or jog
21. Race cars, horses, boats
22. Take a hot bath, sauna, hot tub
23. Play lawn sports (croquet)
24. Bask in the sun
25. Go camping
26. Officiate sports
27. Play a round of golf with friends
28. Dance
29. Others
    Physical Activity Subtotal   _____
    Comments:

3. Intellectual Stimulation Item   Frequency
    1. Study religion, philosophies of life
    2. Study art and the classics
    3. Learn a new management skill
    4. Read newspapers and magazines
    5. Attend professional conferences
    6. Take short courses, workshops
    7. Read professional journals
    8. Engage in thoughtful conversation
    9. Read self-improvement books
   10. Travel for personal enrichment
   11. Attend cultural events
   12. Study for advanced degree/certification
       Intellectual Subtotal   _____
       Comments:

4. Entertainment Item   Frequency
    1. Watch television
    2. Go to a museum, art exhibit
    3. Go to a movie
    4. Go to a play, theatrical performance
    5. Take a week or longer vacation
    6. Have a quiet lunch alone

7. Eat out at a restaurant   Frequency
8. Take a 3-day weekend
9. Take a ride to the country
10. Attend a concert
11. Go to the mountains, beach, lake
12. Patronize a bar, nightclub
13. Go to the zoo, circus, fair
14. Have a picnic, barbecue
15. Watch people
16. Build and watch a cozy fire
17. Watch a sporting event
18. Read a book, novel, short story
19. Read comics, cartoons, humorous books
20. Others
    Entertainment Subtotal   _____
    Comments:

5. Personal Interests Item   Frequency
    1. Play a musical instrument
    2. Can, freeze, make preservatives
    3. Care for houseplants
    4. Refurbish furniture, cars, antiques
    5. Work around the house
    6. Train dogs, horses, pets
    7. Write creative stories, poems
    8. Gamble
    9. Work on crafts
    10. Work in the arts (painting, drawing,
        photography)
    11. Collect coins, stamps
    12. Take a special interest class
    13. Gardening
    14. Have a drink
    15. Cook gourmet meals
    16. Take nature walks
    17. Others
        Personal Interests Subtotal   _____
        Comments:

6. Managerial Item   Frequency

    1. Attend informal staff meetings
    2. Share problems/decisions with colleagues
    3. Help staff with personal problems
    4. Train staff for professional growth
    5. Screen calls, drop-in visitors
    6. Attend professional development seminar
    7. Delegate responsibility
    8. Praise a job well done
    9. Hire competent personnel
  10. Say no
  11. Consolidate similar tasks
  12. Talk to faculty/staff for advice
  13. Avoid the cluttered desk syndrome
  14. Ask faculty/staff for feedback
  15. Give faculty/staff helpful feedback
  16. Work to finish task, leave with clear mind
  17. Reduce meeting time
  18. Set professional goals
  19. Don't make snap decisions
  20. Complete tasks of priority
  21. Change pace of activity
  22. Handle each piece only once
  23. Find the humor in crisis
  24. Share experiences with others
  25. Don't procrastinate
  26. Read professional journals
  27. Take time to plan
  28. Leave work an hour early
  29. Do one task at a time
  30. Communicate clearly
  31. Take short breaks
  32. Chip away at large important tasks
  33. Others
      Managerial Subtotal   _____
      Comments:

7. Attitudes Item   Frequency
  1. Keep weekends free of office work
  2. Resolve problems immediately
  3. Analyze how time is spent
  4. Take time to think
  5. Smile
  6. Leave problems at work
  7. Keep a sense of humor
  8. Laugh at self
  9. Believe in healthy habits
  10. Blow off steam when necessary
  11. Set personal goals
  12. Think about something positive
  13. Recall spiritual supports, pray
  14. Listen to a sermon
  15. Sing by yourself
  16. Establish personal priorities
  17. Be well prepared
  18. Cry
  19. Remind self of limitations
  20. Accept what can't be changed
  21. Have confidence to meet challenges
  22. Realize responsibility for own behavior
  23. Look for positive in people
  24. View crisis in perspective
  25. Do the best one can
  26. Find positive aspects of job
  27. Separate ego from issues
  28. Produce quality, not quantity
  29. Share problems and successes
  30. Be optimistic
  31. Seek serenity in life
  32. Know when and when not to strive
     for perfection
  33. Others
     Attitudes Subtotal   _____
     Comments:

Scoring the Coping Response Inventory

The purpose of the CRI is to analyze how you respond to stress. Your scores on the CRI can be interpreted in two ways:

1. the number of coping responses you use, or your CRI Profile

2. the frequency with which you use them.

CRI Profile: You need to first assess how many coping responses you use. To summarize your score, use the CRI Scoring Sheet (Exercise 7.2) that follows. Take the number of responses you have used in each of the categories, subtract this number from the total possible responses in each category, and write the scores in "Total Responses Used." In the last column, write out a prescription for making better use of possible reponses.

Now display your scores so you can graphically see how you are coping. The circular Coping Response Profile (Exercise 7.3) provides you with this visualization. Notice that the concentric circles on the diagram represent percentiles indicating the proportion of total coping responses in each category. Plot your scores from the worksheets onto the profile by placing a mark along each of the eight radii in accordance with your scores in each of the categories. The farther you are out toward the circle's circumference, the greater the percentage of responses you use in that category. Once you are finished plotting your scores on each of the eight radii, connect the eight marks using straight lines. You now have a graphic scheme that portrays the balance of your coping responses. Is your profile full and robust, or are several categories deflated?

Interpreting Your CRI: To interpret your CRI accurately, you must scrutinize both your response profile (the number of coping techniques you use) and your frequency scores. If your response profile is weak in any of the categories, this is the first clue that you may not have as well-balanced a set of coping responses as you could have. For each category that is below 50 percentile, check to see if you have a number of coping responses that you use frequently (weekly to monthly). If not, read through the items never used ("0") and consider them as potential coping techniques to add to your coping repertoire. Select the ones you would consider to be most effective, take your calendar out, and write them in your schedule. Another choice would be to increase the frequency of any coping responses you now use.

Exercise 7.2

CRI Scoring Sheet

(1) Category	(2) Total Responses Used	(3) Prescription
1. Social		
2. Physical		
3. Intellectual		
4. Entertainment		
5. Personal		
6. Managerial		
7. Attitude		

Exercise 7.3

Coping Response Profile

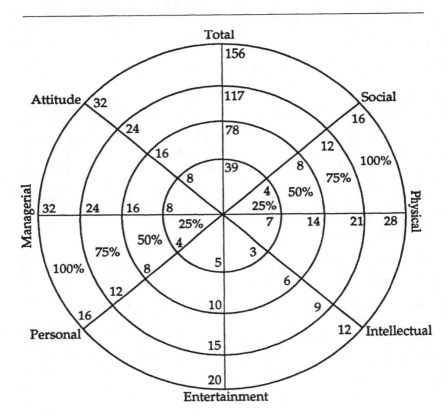

Resource A

Secretarial Stress Index

The following work-related situations have been identified as sources of concern. It is possible that some of these situations bother you more than others. How much are you bothered by each of the situations listed below? Please circle the appropriate response.

	Bothers me				
	Rarely				Frequently
1. Being interrupted frequently by telephone calls	1	2	3	4	5
2. Feeling that I am not fully qualified to handle my job	1	2	3	4	5
3. Waiting to get information needed to carry out my job properly	1	2	3	4	5
4. Thinking that I will not be able to satisfy the conflicting demands of those who have authority over me	1	2	3	4	5

	Bothers me				
	Rarely				Frequently
5. Feeling not enough is expected of me by my superiors	1	2	3	4	5
6. Having my work frequently interrupted by staff members who want to talk	1	2	3	4	5
7. Imposing excessively high expectations on myself	1	2	3	4	5
8. Feeling pressure for better job performance over and above what I think is reasonable	1	2	3	4	5
9. Typing memos, letters, and other communications	1	2	3	4	5
10. Trying to resolve differences with my supervisors	1	2	3	4	5
11. Not knowing what my supervisor thinks of me, or how he/she evaluates my performance	1	2	3	4	5
12. Having to make decisions that affect the lives of others (colleagues, staff members, students)	1	2	3	4	5
13. Feeling I have to participate in work activities at the expense of my personal time	1	2	3	4	5
14. Feeling that I have too much responsibility delegated to me by my supervisors	1	2	3	4	5
15. Trying to get the boss to complete reports and other paperwork on time	1	2	3	4	5
16. Feeling that I have too little authority to carry out responsibilities assigned to me	1	2	3	4	5
17. Feeling that I have too heavy a workload, one that I cannot possibly finish during the normal work day	1	2	3	4	5

			Bothers me		
	Rarely				Frequently

18. Complying with the organizational rules and policies	1	2	3	4	5
19. Feeling that the progress on the job is not what it could be or should be	1	2	3	4	5
20. Being unclear on just what the scope and responsibilities of my job are	1	2	3	4	5
21. Being treated as less important by professional staff	1	2	3	4	5
22. Working in a noisy, disruptive environment	1	2	3	4	5
23. Being bored by routine tasks of my job	1	2	3	4	5
24. Needing to see my boss and not being able to	1	2	3	4	5

Resource B

Secretary-Principal Stressors Profile

Instructions to the manager:

1. List your top 10 stressors (from the Administrative Stress Index), assigning weighted values in Column A from "10" for the most stressful to "1" for the least stressful.
2. Identify your secretary's top 10 stressors (from the Secretarial Stress Index) and assign similar weighted values.
3. In Column B record your secretary's weighted values next to your values. If your secretary has some different stressors than you, list these in the blank spaces below your top 10 stressors.
4. If you have two or three secretaries, repeat steps 2 and 3 and indicate their values in Columns C and D, respectively.
5. Add Columns A and B (C and D if applicable) to arrive at your combined score. Place these scores in the Total column.
6. Rank the combined scores in the final column (Rank), with the highest score receiving a #1 rank, second-highest #2, and so on. You now have a priority listing of Secretary-Principal Stressors.

After this has been completed, the profile can be used as a basis for comments, discussion, and questions between you and your secretary. Ultimately, you will want to resolve these stressors by jointly completing the Principal Action Plan exercises.

Principal's Top 10 Stressors	A	B	C	D	Total	Rank
1.						
2.						
3.						
4.						
5.						
6.						
7.						
8.						
9.						
10						

References

Argyris, C. (1971). *Management and organization development*. New York: McGraw Hill.

Bem, S. L. (1981). The BSRI and gender schema theory: A reply to Spence and Helmreich. *Psychology Review, 88*(4), 369-271.

Bolles, R. N. (1978). *The three boxes of life and how to get out of them.* Berkeley, CA: Ten Speed Press.

Bolles, R. N. (1979). *What color is your parachute?* Berkeley, CA: Ten Speed Press.

Cooper, C. L., & Marshall, J. (1976). Occupational sources of stress: A review of the literature relating to coronary heart disease and mental health. *Journal of Occupational Psychology, 49*, 11-28.

Corwin, R. G. (1969). *A comparative analysis of complex organizations: On power, involvement, and their correlates.* New York: Free Press.

Drucker, P. F. (1967). *The effective executive.* New York: Harper & Row.

Fisher, R., & Ury, W. (1983). *Getting to yes.* New York: Penguin.

Friedman, M., & Rosenman, R. H. (1974). *Type A behavior and your heart.* New York: Knopf.

Gmelch, W. H. (1981). *Release from stress.* Eugene, OR: OSSC Bulletin, Nos. 9 & 10.

Gmelch, W. H. (1982). *Beyond stress to effective management.* New York: John Wiley.

Gmelch, W. H. (1983). Stress for success: How to optimize your performance. *Theory Into Practice, 22*(1), 7-14.

Gmelch, W. H. (1988). Research perspectives on administrative stress: Causes, reactions, responses, and consequences. *The Journal of Educational Administration, 26*(2), 134-140.

Gmelch, W. H., Chan, W., & Torelli, J. A. (1992). *Study of stress in school administration.* Pullman: Center for the Study of Department Chairs, Washington State University.

Gmelch, W. H., & Miskin, V. D. (1993). *Leadership skills for department chairs.* Boston, MA: Anker Press.

Gmelch, W. H., & Swent, B. (1984). Management team stressors and their impact on adminstrators' health. *Journal of Educational Administration, 22*(2), 192-205.

Kobasa, S., Hilker, R., & Maddi, S. (1979). Psychological hardiness. *Journal of Occupational Medicine, 21,* 595-598.

Mackenzie, R. A. (1990). *The time trap.* New York: AMACOM.

Mager, R. F., & Pipe, P. (1970). *Analyzing peformance problems.* Belmont, CA: Fearon.

Margolis, B. L., Kroes, W. H., & Quinn, R. P. (1974). Job stress: An unlisted occupational hazard. *Journal of Occupational Medicine, 16*(10), 383-397.

Maslach, C., & Jackson, S. E. (1981). The measurement of experienced burnout. *Journal of Occupational Behavior, 2,* 99-113.

McGrath, J. E. (1976a). Stress and behavior in organizations. In M. D. Dunnette (Ed.), *Handbook of industrial and organizational psychology.* Chicago: Rand McNally.

McGrath, J. E. (1976b). Cracking under stress: How executives learn to cope. *U.S. News & World Report, 80*(19), 59-61.

Sargent, A. G. (1981). Training men and women for androgynous behaviors in organizations. *Group & Organization Studies, 6*(3), 302-311.

Selye, H. (1976). *The stress of life.* New York: McGraw Hill.

Siebert, H. (November, 1980). *Working with difficult people.* Seminar, Portland, OR.

Smith, M. J. (1975). *When I say no I feel guilty.* New York: Bantam.

Torelli, J. A., & Gmelch, W. H. (1993). Occupational stress and burnout in educational administration. *People and Education, 4.* (1), 363-381.
Yankelovich, Skelley, & White (1982). In W. H. Gmelch (Ed.), *Beyond stress to effective management.* New York: John Wiley.

Index